"In *Wait—Is This Racist? A Guide to Becoming an Antiracist Church*, you have before you a guidebook, a survival guide, a deconstruction chisel, and a faithful interpretation of the reign of God that is at hand. This book made me think critically about my own blind spots while also acknowledging the potential areas of growth that could happen in my personal and professional life. The book masterfully offers a clarion call to embrace a God who unites rather than the idol of white supremacy that divides. You would be wise to sit with this book—it will change you."
— Robert W. Lee, pastor and author of *A Sin by Any Other Name: Reckoning with Racism and the Heritage of the South*

"*Wait—Is This Racist?* is a practical guide to the work that so many white Christians feel paralyzed by in our churches: how to examine the lingering presence of white supremacy culture in our ministry practices and where to turn for tangible ways of untangling ourselves from it. The authors draw on a wealth of experience to help churches prepare for and navigate the journey toward freedom from the lie of whiteness, and their wisdom is essential guidance for those of us who are looking for a way forward."
—Chris Furr, author of *Straight White Male: A Faith-Based Guide to Deconstructing Your Privilege and Living with Integrity*

"Wow. Read this book right now and tell everyone involved in church to read this book. Then use it as the thorough-yet-concise, accessible, practical handbook that it is to help your church not only *do* anti-racism work but *become* anti-racist. The book is a perfect combination of theory and practice, and it manages to do in one volume what previously has required using multiple resources and piecing something together to move forward. There's nothing else out there quite like it. This book has the power to change us for good."
—Jaime Clark-Soles, Professor of New Testament, Perkins School of Theology

"Whether you are contemplating or are already in the process of making systemic changes toward racial equity in your church, this book is for you. Transparent, engaging, and at times disruptive, *Wait—Is This Racist?* is a practical guide that helps you and your leadership team ask all the right questions about every aspect of your church, moving you beyond performative allyship to genuine transformation."
—Sari Ateek, rector, St. John's Episcopal Church, Norwood Parish, Chevy Chase, Maryland

"The white Christian church in America has blood on her hands for conflating white supremacy with the church—a violent truth many churches aren't willing to face and one that didn't happen only in the past but that continues today. *Wait—Is this Racist?* is a necessary stop in any white congregation's road in the soul work of anti-racism."

—Amanda Hambrick Ashcraft, executive minister, Middle Collegiate Church, New York City, and founder of Raising Imagination

"The progressive church preaches and performs anti-racism. However, it's incredibly rare to find the church that invests in being anti-racist and divesting their privilege. *Wait—Is This Racist?* is a powerful, uncomfortable, and necessary challenge to dismantle the systems of whiteness in our churches. It's the perfect guide for those who are ready to get serious about embodying an anti-racist gospel."

—Jonathan Williams, author of *She's My Dad: A Father's Transition and a Son's Redemption* and founder of Forefront Brooklyn

"*Wait—Is This Racist? A Guide to Becoming an Anti-Racist Church* is an incredibly powerful tool and a work of collaborative art. The teaching, suggested practices, and deep wisdom in these pages are tailor-made for all churches that want to be a part of this work of anti-racism—this work that is so vital to the good news that the incarnate Jesus brings to us today. As a pastor committed to leading an anti-racist church, I am eager to begin using this resource in my own community. I can't recommend it any more highly to fellow church leaders and clergy."

—Amanda Rigby, Associate Pastor for Discipleship and Youth, The Peak Church, Apex, North Carolina

Wait—Is This Racist?

Wait—Is This Racist?

A Guide to Becoming
an Anti-Racist Church

KERRY CONNELLY

with
Bryana Clover
and
Josh Riddick

WESTMINSTER
JOHN KNOX PRESS
LOUISVILLE · KENTUCKY

First edition
Published by Westminster John Knox Press
Louisville, Kentucky

22 23 24 25 26 27 28 29 30 31—10 9 8 7 6 5 4 3 2 1

Unless otherwise indicated, Scripture quotations are from the New Revised Standard Version of the Bible, copyright © 1989 by the Division of Christian Education of the National Council of the Churches of Christ in the U.S.A., and are used by permission.

Book design by Drew Stevens
Cover design by Marc Whitaker / MTWdesign.net
Cover photo: Kumar Sriskandan / Alamy Stock Photo

Library of Congress Cataloging-in-Publication Data

Names: Connelly, Kerry, author. | Clover, Bryana, author. | Riddick, Josh, author.
Title: Wait–is this racist? : a guide to becoming an anti-racist church / Kerry Connelly with Bryana Clover and Josh Riddick.
Description: First edition. | Louisville, Ky. : Westminster John Knox Press, 2022. | Includes bibliographical references. | Summary: "A "be-it-yourself" guide to anti-racism for churches that examines all operations of church life so that churches and church leaders can create a workable action plan to truly become more justice-oriented organizations"-- Provided by publisher.
Identifiers: LCCN 2021055852 (print) | LCCN 2021055853 (ebook) | ISBN 9780664267506 (paperback) | ISBN 9781646982417 (ebook)
Subjects: LCSH: Racism--Religious aspects--Christianity. | Race relations--Religious aspects--Christianity. | Anti-racism--United States. | Church.
Classification: LCC BT734 .C59 2022 (print) | LCC BT734 (ebook) | DDC 277.3/082089--dc23
LC record available at https://lccn.loc.gov/2021055852
LC ebook record available at https://lccn.loc.gov/2021055853

Most Westminster John Knox Press books are available at special quantity discounts when purchased in bulk by corporations, organizations, and special-interest groups. For more information, please e-mail SpecialSales@wjkbooks.com.

Contents

Author's Note

As a White woman working in the space of anti-racism, I receive a lot of critique from a lot of people. This is not surprising, and the accountability is a good thing. There is a specific critique I'd like to address here that's very important, and it's one I take very seriously: is it OK to be a White woman who gets paid for doing anti-racism work? I want to address this directly and with the nuance it deserves, because it is an excellent question. Within the White, cis-hetero patriarchy, my embodiment holds a number of identities, including my identities as both a White person (dominance) and a woman (not always dominant). This makes this question dicey.

On the one hand, White people getting paid to do anti-racism work seems obscene, because we are now merely finding a new, warm and fuzzy way to profit off of marginalized communities and our own White saviorism. On the other hand, women's labor has often been undervalued and expected. We are socialized into believing that our work, our intellectual property, our emotional labor should be offered to the world for the taking. (This is exponentially true for BIPOC women.) Resisting the devaluation of our labor is an intensive emotional struggle that starts within our own psyches. Only then can we do the terrifying job of asking for what we are actually worth in the marketplace. When one woman insists on getting paid for her labor, it is a bold act of resistance and liberation for all women.

I've spent a lot of time discerning whether White people even have a place in this work and have arrived at the unequivocal answer that yes, we absolutely do. It is, after all, the wounded White soul that is doing all this harm; we need White leaders to accompany White people through the journey of their identity deconstruction, and imaginative visionaries to help us find a new way to be White in the world. To that end, my work in studying Whiteness as a construct and inviting the collective into a new imagination continues, and I also willingly seek out and submit to accountability to my BIPOC siblings.

For a very long time, I did this work for free. I wrote blog posts that produced more death threats than dollars, and I engaged in far more social media debates than I care to remember. I spent years in seminary studying Black Liberation and Womanist theologies, and the few times I was invited to speak on the topic, I often did so for free and paid my way to the event to boot. And I can't even tell you how many White guys have slid into my DMs asking for some personalized instruction in how to be anti-racist (which they mostly ignored, by the way). Since the release of my book *Good White Racist?*, however, things have changed. Though I still receive requests to write and work for free, there are more and more opportunities to use my training as a coach and a consultant in more meaningful and impactful ways, and those ways are often paid gigs. So, how to do this work ethically while also supporting myself and my family and resisting the narrative that women's work should be offered for free? Here is my commitment:

First, I vocally and ardently support a national reparations movement. Trust me when I say that my income would not make even a dent in the huge debt owed to the Black community to repair the economic devastation that pseudosupremacy has caused. What is more important is our collective repentance, and that must include financial reparations. There are many creative ways to do this, imagined by people much smarter than me. We will, of course, offer many ideas in this book, but we also invite you to imagine with us. This book will challenge church leaders to lean into the divestment of your resources for the purpose of imaginative reparations, but this is only the start.

Second, I commit to tithe on any income I receive for anti-racism work to BIPOC-led organizations that support BIPOC flourishing. This includes the income generated from this book. (In some cases in the past, I have given away 100 percent of my profit, but that is not sustainable.) I state this because I think it is important to model this to other White people in this work and so you know I have some skin in this game personally. However, this will be one of the very few places I talk about it, because parading my own financial contributions—small as they may be—feels performative and gross. I am trying to balance the need to address this concern and demonstrate how important this is with the need to just shut up about it and do it quietly, which is also important. This isn't about performing White goodness—or my goodness—it's about doing what's right.

Third, I resist celebrity culture by insisting on shared platforms, and commit to using my platform to lift up BIPOC whenever possible. I learned about resisting celebrity culture from Dr. Robyn Henderson-Espinoza, who models it beautifully. Before my bestie Aisha rolls her eyes at me, I'm not saying I'm a celebrity—that's actually a really funny thought. What I am saying is that our culture loves to put some people on highly visible pedestals while other important voices don't get heard at all. If and when I get offered a pedestal—even a short, stubby one—I will boldly take my place there and use my voice to resist the silencing of women, and my commitment is to bring BIPOC with me when I do it.

Fourth, I commit to staying in my own lane. My work concerns the deconstruction of Whiteness and the companioning of White people on their journey of racial awakening. My work is *not* about "helping" BIPOC (White saviorism) and it is certainly not about speaking for BIPOC. I don't get to co-opt the Black and Brown experience in my work. While my work obviously intersects with their stories, I will always give attribution and credit. If I miss something, I commit to fixing that as soon as it is brought to my attention.

Finally, thank you for the chance to speak into this incredibly important subject. Lives are at stake, so let's get to work.

Love,
Kerry
West Orange, NJ
April 17, 2021

Acknowledgments

Kerry

A project like this does not happen in a vacuum, and I would not be equipped to do this work if it were not for the multitudes of BIPOC voices who continue to cry out for justice. Their willingness to teach White people about ourselves—even in the face of our stubborn denial—is heroic. I am not just thinking of the current voices you may already be reading. I am thinking of the ancestral souls that cried out for justice as they were loaded like cargo onto death-trap ships, stolen from their families and their homeland. I am grateful for the opportunity to hear their cries and to respond, and perhaps offer an ounce of repentance and reparation in a sea of despair. To that end, I dedicate this book to the individuals who have haunted me since I first learned about them while writing *Good White Racist?*: the two young African boys who were offered as a tithe to the church by the slave trader Prince Henry of Portugal. May you forgive us, and rest easy.

I am so eternally grateful to Josh and Bryana, my collaborators on this book who brought important lessons, wisdom, and power to its pages. You birthed this baby with me, and I am so grateful for your gracious willingness to educate and teach. Your voices are important. Thank you.

A huge thank you to our editor, Jessica Miller Kelley, whose keen eye makes the work just So. Much. Better. Thank you for noticing my work, thank you for lifting it up, and thank you for improving it. And to the entire team at WJK, who have been so supportive and encouraging—you've made my dreams of being a writer come true *and* made it an amazing process to boot. Thank you!

I need to give a shout-out to my preacher camp friends—this amazing group of people I met and traveled with in seminary who have been cheerleaders, friends, coconspirators, and make me finally feel like a cool kid even though we all know I am inherently weird. Here's to you, Anne, Ben, Cassidy, Jennifer, Jen, Mason, Melissa, TJ, Shaleen, and

Simone. Thank you for loving me anyway. And Kay, for letting me crash in Indy, even after I let your cat out.

As always, Nicole and Aisha, I have the glitter. When do we roll? Who will invite Bart?

Of course, Michael, who folds more than his share of laundry and loads more dishes into the dishwasher than is probably fair, needs massive kudos for making this possible. Thank you for your love and encouragement and reminding me to believe in myself. I love you.

It always comes down to the future, though. To that end, thank you to my beautiful, amazing children, Delaney and Evan. I love who you are and who you are becoming. Thank you for being the force in the world that will make oppressive systems shudder with fear when they see you coming. I see you, and I love you.

Bryana

Collaborating on this book was one of the hardest and most rewarding experiences for me. It was also unexpectedly therapeutic for me to put my experiences and thoughts out into the hands of unknown readers. None of this would have been possible without my coach, business partner, and friend, Kerry. I always dreamed of writing a book one day, but it seemed like a distant dream until she proposed the idea for *Wait—Is This Racist?* Our friendship has helped me to realize what a healthy relationship with a White person looks like. She inspires me to always speak my truth, because my voice matters, which is one of the greatest gifts I've received from a friend.

I'm eternally grateful to my husband, Troy, who read my chapter drafts, kept food on the table, and did nap times, bedtimes, and play-times with our sweet Emmett so that I could write whenever I felt inspired (which often required a lot of encouraging nudges). He is my best friend and my biggest fan. He is the perfect balance to my busy mind and the greatest supporter of my wild ideas.

To Pastor José Luis Villaseñor, who took a chance on me and was my first paid client to do race equity work within the church. He saw me. He shared in my pain. He trusted me. He inspired me to speak my truth.

To Rev. Katey Zeh, my soul-sister-friend, who lit a fire within me to pay attention to Spirit nudges, and to lean into my spiritual curiosity to find my truth. Thank you for the middle-of-the-night Voxer talks, and for showing me the beauty of true friendship. Our sisterhood helped give me the strength and confidence I needed to put words to paper.

To all the intelligent and creative Black sister-friends of Maya's Room (and the beautiful Margaret Brunson who brought me in) for loving me, encouraging me, and creating space for me even before meeting me in person (COVID, y'all). These beautiful women lit a fire within me to confidently say and to believe: "I am a writer."

To my family. To my best friend and sister, Ally: for the daily texts and FaceTimes and your unconditional love. To my little brother, Mac: thank you for your humor and wisdom, and for always challenging me. To my mom and dad: thank you for embracing the awkward family Zooms where I would ask random questions about being raised biracial and handling them with grace.

To my ancestors, of blood and of spirit, who come to me in my dreams, when I'm meditating, and who are even there when I'm too busy to notice. My intention is to honor you in everything that I do. *I am* because of your sacrifice.

Finally, I want to thank all of my "teachers" who have mentored me, challenged me, and encouraged me. I listened, and it meant something.

Josh

Being able to create alongside Kerry and Bry has been one of the great joys of this pandemic year. I'm honored to share my voice, experience, and expertise through this book. The process of writing, revising, and rewriting is profoundly spiritual and vulnerable. I am deeply grateful for Kerry and Bry's vulnerability in their writing, which inspires me to be more vulnerable both in ways you'll read in the book and in how I show up in the world.

I cannot thank my family enough for giving me the time and space needed to bring my torrent of thoughts into meaningful words. Linds, thank you for gracefully helping me process the harm we've experienced in faith spaces as I wrote and for always being a thought partner through all my writer's block. Words can't capture how much I love the life we have crafted together. Jade and Xolani, you both are too young to understand what this book means (let alone be able to read it), but one day you will. I want you to know how thankful I am for both of you. Your presence of laughter, screams, and everything in between serves as a constant reminder of who I am crafting a better world for. You don't know it yet, but you both constantly teach me to embody joy and play as acts of resistance in a world set on plundering our joy. You both are helping liberate me.

Thank you, Dasha Saintremy and Matthew Mosley, for contributing your voices to this book. You both are family to me and have been consistent voices of encouragement and love. I love y'all. Thank you to the cloud of witnesses that offered encouragement and challenged me to keep looking deeper: Ben Tapper, Hazel Owens, Cameron Davis, Joseph Edmunds, Manon Voice, Lashawnda Crowe, and Melyssa Cordero. Every one of you continues to help me have a more beautiful and expansive imagination of what our world can be. Thank you for loving me, thank you for loving *us*!

Thank you to the ancestors and elders, those I know and those I do not. Your struggle has given me the breath to speak of liberation in a way that I hope makes you proud.

Introduction

The question always comes, eventually.

Whether it's after a talk I've just done, at a church with which I'm consulting, or when I'm speaking one-on-one with someone, White people, ultimately, always want to know the answer to one specific question: "What can we actually *do* about racism?" I sense the good intentions here, the real desire to fix a problem to which they are either just awakening or with which they have struggled for some time. I hear the deep desire to do better. I also sense some desperation—a response to being overwhelmed, a desire to be good, and a real craving for a quick fix to a very complicated situation.

Tell me what to do to not be racist anymore, and I'll just do it. Check the box. Push the button. Post to Instagram. Task complete.

It's an understandable phenomenon. After all, the Protestant work ethic teaches us that we must work our way into God's grace and a state of goodness, rather than finding beauty and worthiness in our very embodiment. Capitalism tells us we must be productive and that our value is variable based on market demand, rather than our inherent human worth. Technology teaches us that our results must be instant. When combined with Whiteness, these paradigms spur us into a frenzy of do-gooder action and White saviorism, where we rush to offer tutoring to struggling students of color or fly across the ocean to go on mission trips to feed hungry bellies on other continents. To be clear, White saviorism is nothing new—it's been around for a long time,

1

but modern technology seems to add a certain frenetic, social-justice-warrior, meme-filled energy to it.

All of this raises the question—do we want to be anti-racist because that's what the current market demands? Or because we long for the true shalom of God and know it can't exist without real racial justice? It's an important question, and the answer will result in radically different behaviors. While I am encouraged by the recent rush of desire among White people to *do something* after the horrific murders of George Floyd, Ahmaud Arbery, and Breonna Taylor, the real danger here is a justice that is only **performative**—one that makes White people feel great about ourselves but doesn't initiate any real change. Still, I believe that as institutions that have a huge influence on the spiritual formation and worldview of individuals as well as deep cultural and community impact, churches have the potential to be a massive influence for justice in our world. If—and that's a big *if*—we are willing to actually engage in a **divestment of power.** (Note that words in bold are explained more fully in the glossary starting on page 181.)

Churches are used to being charitable; when it comes to responding to the world's physical needs, the church is an expert at feeding empty bellies and clothing cold bodies. Charitable efforts that feed and care for the marginalized are, of course, important and worthy. After all, cold bodies need clothes, and hungry bellies need food. When it comes to racial justice, however, very often the work White people rush through in order to feel as if we are *doing something* is ineffective, and sometimes it even does more harm than good. We might post to social media or even join a protest. We may attend book clubs and read Black authors. We may even work to extend our social circle, our musical tastes, our electoral choices in the voting booth. These things are important, but they are nowhere near enough. We are Doing the Right Things, and this is good, but until we begin to initiate real change by *divesting ourselves of power and privilege,* nothing will actually change. Worse, our performance of justice without real change can lead to the dangerous complacency associated with the belief that posting to social media means that we have *done something* and are therefore existentially anti-racist.

So, what does it mean to actually divest ourselves of power and privilege? This can manifest in many ways, and it is the imaginative edge that I am inviting you to dance along with me. This is the work of White labor: to imagine new ways to be White in the world that not only do no harm, but also participate in collective liberation. This book will give you some ideas as a jumping-off point, but you are invited to bring your genesis, your creativity, your imagination to the work as well. More importantly, you and I together are invited to submit to the imaginations of the **BIPOC** community as they give us feedback on our Whiteness and how to be better human beings. This cuts to the core problem of Whiteness: we think we know what's best for everyone, including us.

This may surprise you, but Jesus is a pretty good example of someone who divested himself of power. According to the Christian narrative, Jesus had the power of the Almighty at his fingertips, and never once did he use it for his own gain. When Jesus did use his access to divine resources, every single time it was focused on helping someone else. Not once did Jesus say, I need a building, so I will manifest some gold to pay for it. Not once did Jesus say, these Romans are hurting my feelings, so I will persecute them with legislation. Even when Jesus was actually being persecuted by both a mob and the state, he did not call down what must have been some pretty awesome smiting powers. No—he called down forgiveness and grace. When he saw hungry bellies he fed them, but he also healed bodies and restored them to community; he banqueted with the marginalized and called them his siblings and his friends; he resisted systems of power, ultimately spreading his arms wide to demonstrate power's murderous sin. There is no greater statement of condemnation for power than the cross.

There are still some White churches who resist saying that Black lives actually do matter. This statement, they claim, is too political. Give them a hungry belly, and they'll feed it, believing that this is what Jesus would do. They are not wrong—I think he would, too. But there is a disconnect in these White churches between the hungry belly and the body politic that creates it, and a lack of understanding that the church can—and has a responsibility to—impact both. Since the time that Jesus had a body that walked on this earth, the church has changed dramatically, becoming an institution imbued with the very type of power Jesus resisted.

Charitable programs implemented by institutions that hold power are important. But they can *also* run the risk of making White folk feel self-satisfied, as if we can check the boxes and be deemed *totally not racist* because we ventured into the inner city to mentor at-risk youth, and most of them happened to be Black. This is the act of "doing" anti-racism, and at best, it's a short-term solution to a systemic problem. This book will help you engage in some of the deep paradigm shifts that are necessary for your church to become an organization that doesn't just *do* anti-racism, but actually *is* anti-racist—from the inside out.

While we are busying ourselves with feeding hungry bellies and protesting state-sanctioned violence, we *also* need to be addressing the systems that cause them—and that includes interrogating the ones we ourselves perpetuate and participate in as institutions that hold power. That means looking at the way we think about poverty, education, and taxes. It includes things like property ownership and capitalism, public domain, overpoliced communities of color, "law and order" politicians, and "good side of the tracks" mentalities. We need to interrogate the bootstrap ideology, and we need to recognize whether we deem people worthy by their societal productivity or simply by the fact that they are human (your answer may surprise you). And we need to identify the ways in which our beliefs in these areas infiltrate the way we do church.

If we are only willing to do the easy work of giving up a Saturday afternoon to hand out peanut butter and jelly sandwiches but not willing to sit with the ways we embody **systemic racism** with our votes, the policies we support, or the way we stay silent when racist Uncle Joe tells us his fifteen millionth bad joke, we are not *being* anti-racist, we are *performing* anti-racism. If we are only willing to entertain notions of anti-racism that make us totally comfortable and feel familiar, we are not *being* anti-racist, we are *doing* anti-racism. And anti-racism that is only *performed* or *done* and not embodied and internalized is not really anti-racism at all. In fact, it teeters on the side of racist White saviorism at best. At worst, it's straight-up racist tomfoolery wrapped up in a blanket of White warm fuzzies.

As churches and institutions work to become more anti-racist in our being, a five-week sermon series or a book-group discussion about work by a Black author is not enough. Those are important parts of becoming, but not the entirety of a holistic state of being anti-racist. Institutions that seek to become existentially anti-racist—to have anti-racism be something they *are,* rather than something they *do*—must look at how we show up in the world on a daily basis, not just during Black History Month. How do we honor the land we are on and the people who once inhabited it? How do we resist **White pseudosupremacy** in our daily operations? How do we consistently interrogate narratives that maintain the racist status quo? What is our response when we identify ways in which we have done or do harm to Black and Brown communities? How do we embody lament and reparations? How do the ways in which we use language or music or policy or any other number of things that happen, automatically perpetuate that which we hope to resist? These are not easy questions and there are no simple answers.

The point is that if we focus our efforts less on doing and more on becoming, the right doing will come from our becoming. The work toward which we must endeavor is to be comfortable with the fact that a truly just society looks nothing like what we currently have. This is a terrifying notion to many of us, but this is because we have yet to start imagining, to lean into the power of our own genesis and creative being to envision something new. There is an imaginative void that is ours to fill. White people must ready ourselves to lay down our false dominance and endeavor with the collective, trusting that, as John Franke says in my all-time favorite description of the realm of God, when we reach that holy place of shalom, "Everyone will have enough, and no one needs to be afraid."[1]

HOW TO USE THIS BOOK

This book is designed to be a tool that will help you interrogate the way your organization currently embodies church, identify ways in which those operations, procedures, and liturgies may be propping up White pseudosupremacy, and make the types of structural changes that can effect long-term corporate change. Our goal is nothing short of a world that is just for all creation, and this must begin with our own organizations and our dedication to being existentially anti-racist. As a White person, I am your companion and your guide on this journey. I come to you with a deep understanding of the sense of overwhelm, grief, frustration, and desire you might experience as a White leader who wants to make this right. I know what it's like to have to deconstruct your own identity, to have to find a new way to be in the world. And I'm here to tell you straight up: if you're not feeling uncomfortable, you're doing it wrong.

Of course, one of the hallmarks of White saviorism is when we White people think we know exactly how to fix everything. So while I am completely convinced that White people need to do White work (and I know you're shocked to discover I have some strong opinions about how to do that), and even that we need White leaders leading us in that work, I am also certain that we need to do so under the authority of and in collaboration with members of the BIPOC community.

Addressing racism within our churches is important, impactful work, and we need Black and Brown voices to speak into that process, to illuminate the places where we are unconsciously perpetuating racism, and to help us see how we can be not just inclusive, but truly *anti-racist* in our being. (You may be surprised to know that I do not equate being anti-racist with being more diverse necessarily—but we'll get to that in a bit.) I am also convinced—in fact, I think it's fairly obvious—that creating a more just world is the work of the collective. It's not just White people's work, but rather labor that White people must do in collaboration with—and yes, even in submission to—voices that have traditionally been marginalized. The goal is for the world to no longer be White, with everyone else just doing their best to assimilate, but rather a beautiful coalition of cultures where everyone is valued and thriving in the authenticity of their God-given identities. The new creation—the kin-dom of God—will be the result of all of us imagining something entirely different *together*.

To that end, I am thrilled to introduce you to Bryana Clover and Josh Riddick, two professionals who regularly work with churches—specifically around race issues—who will share their own expertise, stories, and experiences. You'll find their words woven through each chapter, offering invaluable perspectives on each area of church life we'll be discussing. If you are a member of the BIPOC community and leading anti-racist work in primarily White spaces, Bryana and Josh will offer you tips, support, and encouragement from their own wisdom and experiences doing this work. If you're White, you'll learn more about the experiences of Black and Brown people and the emotional labor they must do to navigate White spaces, and you'll also learn how you can better show care and support for them as well.

UNLEARNING WHITENESS

(Bryana)

The labor of unlearning is not easy. It requires sacrifice from all involved, both White people and BIPOC. Guilt is a common emotion that often surfaces for White people, and I want to address this for a moment in the context of anti-racism. For most of us, guilt acts like cancer—slowly and invisibly doing its harm until our sickness catches us by surprise. It paralyzes us into inaction and overwhelms us into a state of shame and despair. When guilt manifests in this way, it causes individual and collective harm. So how can we move from a state of guilt to authentic action? You're reading this book, and that's a great start! I want to provide a quick perspective on culture and socialization that can serve as a tool for you throughout your journey.

In their book titled *Is Everyone Really Equal?*, Özlem Sensoy and Robin DiAngelo provide a helpful paradigm to understand the way culture—and our position within it—impacts our racial identity.[2] According to the authors, each one of us is born into a particular culture. **Culture** essentially encompasses the norms, values, practices, patterns of communication, language, laws, customs, and meanings shared by a group of people in a given time and place. There are obvious elements of a particular culture, such as food or music, but many other elements of culture are more difficult to name. Sensoy and DiAngelo point out that because we are all born into a particular culture, it is often impossible for us to distinguish our own reality *within* our culture from the realities *outside* our culture. These deeper levels of culture include body language, concepts of beauty, and patterns of handling emotions. **Socialization** refers to our "systematic training into the norms of our culture . . . the process of learning the meanings and practices that enable us to make sense of and behave appropriately in that culture."[3] In order for us to engage in the work of anti-racism, it is important for us to recognize how our own position in society shapes what we can see and understand about the world. This is commonly referred to as **positionality**, or social location.

So what does this have to do with guilt, you might ask? One of the ideologies inherent in Western culture is **individualism**—which Sensoy and DiAngelo describe as "the belief that we are each unique and outside the forces of socialization."[4] This is especially ingrained in the psyche of anyone who has spent a majority of their life in the United States. Guilt, therefore, stems from this idea that we are personally responsible for racism—that racism is an ideology that we, as individuals, either hold or do not.

So here is the paradigm shift we wish to introduce: What happens if we recognize racism as a systemic problem and a product of our socialization, rather than merely an individual ideology? What if we can see more clearly how our position in a society that benefits a particular race at the expense of others gives some of us the power and privilege needed to actually dismantle racism? What if we recognize that racism is a collective burden that we all must dismantle with intention, and that it is imperative for our collective liberation? As you engage in the following chapters, take note of when that emotion of guilt creeps in, and make a conscious decision now to challenge that guilt with knowledge and growth.

WHITE SELF-LOVE, GUILT, AND SHAME
(Josh)

One of the practices I use when facilitating interracial workshop groups is taking some time to go around the room for folks to share what they love about their racial identity. It's a fun exercise that gives BIPOC a chance to name parts of themselves that give them joy instead of only being asked to rehash moments of discrimination and marginalization. The answers are usually something like these:

> I love our hair.

> I love our food.

> Oh, I love our creativity and our rhythm.

Smiles light up faces as people get to share what is special about their identity and culture. Then, I arrive at a White participant who squirms uncomfortably in their chair and does not have a response on hand like most of the BIPOC participants. Sometimes I might hear, "I like not being pulled over by the police, I guess?" Every time, White participants in the room struggle to answer that question. Ultimately the participant gives up and acknowledges they do not have anything they love about being White.

White pseudosupremacy has malformed all of us, and as you will learn from this book, White folks are not immune. If you are White, anti-racism work is not just about learning to unbind the oppressed and deconstruct systems, it is also about learning to love yourself—your *White* self. Reclaiming your identity and the capacity to love yourself apart from the powers and privileges of Whiteness is an intimate part of your liberation. Reclaiming your ethnic lineage is one way this can be done—celebrating the perseverance of your Irish immigrant heritage or the robust flavors of the Italian culinary tradition. Doing so enables you not only to (re)discover parts of yourself and your cultural narrative that inform who you are, but also to grapple with how parts of your lineage were erased as the "price of the ticket" into Whiteness. As you hold the guilt Bryana named above, do not let it derail you from the liberative work of learning what it means to love your White identity while still pursuing racial equity.

Guilt is a familiar feeling for White folks who do this work. Learning to identify the emotions that come with guilt and differentiate it from shame is paramount to being able to experience liberation and self-love needed for racial justice to work well. Guilt arises when one becomes aware of behavior or involvement in a system of oppression. Guilt dredges up emotions that White folks tend to avoid but can be great motivators toward pursuing equity. Sitting with the feeling of guilt instead of fleeing or shrinking from it will help you identify where you may have caused harm or made a **microaggression**.

Shame, on the other hand, speaks to our identities and our being. Shame seeks to devalue personhood because of an external action or behavior. Shame undermines our ability to see ourselves as members of the beloved family of God. If you cannot begin to love yourself as you were created, you cannot love others as they were made. BIPOC do not want or need your shame, nor are they responsible for removing that guilt or shame.

For too many White folks, the shame of Whiteness is the motivator to engage in racial justice work. But shame as motivation is unsustainable and unable to help you arrive at a place of loving self. Instead, let your liberation journey be bound up in learning to love how the Divine made you and not how Whiteness shapes you.

ABOUT THIS BOOK

This book is designed to be interactive. In other words, it's not your typical weekend sofa read. It's meant to be a thing you work through both individually and with your fellow church leaders. You'll answer (that is, struggle with) questions and dig deeper to find uncomfortable truths. Just as if Bryana, Josh, or I were coaching you one-on-one, if you really engage the work, you'll find that we won't let you off the hook, and this is the exact thing you need. The questions are designed to bring you deeper so that both you and your organization can travel on the journey from racial awakening, through the deep midnight of the soul that is White grief and lament, to the other side, which is the good and holy work of true liberation for all God's children.

Each chapter will begin with an exploration of why the topic at hand matters. What actually makes it important, for example, to audit the lyrics of your hymns, or consider the way your organization uses space? Unless you understand *why* congregational singing, for example, impacts our worldview, you'll continue to do things the way you always have. That's just human nature. Then, each chapter will take you into a more practical conversation specific to your church's operations before offering you questions you can use with your leadership team to dive deep into an examination of your own organization. It might be helpful for you to go through this as individuals, and then bring your entire staff and/or lay leadership team together to discuss what you've learned and, most importantly, develop a plan of action. The final chapter will help you do just that. You'll look back over the work you've done and use it to complete a strategy for moving forward.

It's important to remember, however, that this is not a one-and-done kind of thing. This is work that will be an ongoing process, a constant awareness and intentionality that you'll need to practice. Remember: this is about becoming, and a way of being. It is not something you "do." Come back to the book regularly to remind yourself of what you've learned, and plan regular check-ins with yourself to examine and interrogate your own identity as a White person. This is a practice that will yield deep and rich results.

Finally, there are a few key points to remember, in no particular order:

This will be messy. Becoming and being an anti-racist church will never be neat and orderly, nor will it ever be complete. You will not reach a singular point in time at which you can effectively say, "We are done." It is contextual, and the anti-racist lexicon is changing daily. It will require you to be agile and able to respond depending on the circumstance. The sooner you understand this, the less painful the process will be.

You will feel resistance. Because this will require a divestment of centralized privilege and power, you will feel uncomfortable. The resistance will come both from within you and from the people around you as you begin to externalize your new, anti-racist stance. This is practically guaranteed. If you don't feel resistance, you're either not doing it right, or you are a White person who has already completely divested from Whiteness. That means I should probably be learning from you. White anti-racism is an exercise in discomfort, and the sooner we all get comfortable with that, the better.

It will require a divestment of resources. Performative anti-racism is free, but true anti-racism has a cost. Churches that hope to become anti-racist but are not willing to redistribute financial resources, human energy, or liturgical time to the process are only perpetuating the problem, not solving it. If you're thinking this will just be an exercise between you and your journal, think again. This is about taking real action, initiating real redistribution, and making real change.

Beloved aspects of your church and its practices may have to go, and that's OK. People tend to cling to things we love. This is human and natural; it's normal to want to resist change. But sentimentalism cannot come at the cost of our anti-racism, and unfortunately some of the things we love are also deeply embedded in supremacy culture. We'll be talking in these chapters about church buildings and imagery, about beloved liturgical practices and the ways we do small groups. You can be almost certain that somewhere, there will be an aspect of the way you do church that is complicated and messy because it is both easy to love and be attached to, and also really racist. You may feel complicated feelings around this yourself, and perhaps more difficult, you'll receive pushback (sometimes, very vehement pushback) from your congregants. But it's important to be merciless and objective here and remember that White feelings are not more important than Black lives, and it is Black lives that are quite literally in danger in the supremacist culture we are working to resist.

It's all based in the White cis-hetero patriarchy. I've met with church leaders who say they want to lead their church toward a more anti-racist stance, but they don't want to use the word *race*.[5] These same churches also refuse to affirm women in leadership roles or the LGBTQ+ community at all. I am adamant that you cannot affirm only one part of a person's identity. If a Black gay woman walks into your church, you cannot tell her that you will love and fight for her Blackness, while refusing to acknowledge her leadership gifts because she is a woman or her spouse because she is attracted to the same sex. **Intersectionality** is important, and you must be willing to engage all of these parts of her identity in meaningful ways. The one thing that racism, patriarchy, and heteronormativity have in common is *power*—a state of being in which the dominant group controls access, influence, and resources. A truly Jesus-centered and anti-racist church will seek to divest itself of power at all costs, even when it feels really uncomfortable.

Diversity is not the goal. When I consult with churches, this is often the first big hurdle I need to help leadership to leap over. Somewhere along the line, Whiteness has taught us that to be successfully *not racist* means that we need to have faces of all different colors sitting in our pews. I'm here to tell you that diversity should *not* be the goal of your anti-racism work, and I'll go even further to say that diversity efforts usually do more harm to the BIPOC community than good. You can be a really awesome, wholly anti-racist church and still be completely White, all at the same time. In fact, a key aspect of being anti-racist is recognizing that sometimes, the BIPOC community just needs BIPOC-only spaces, because Whiteness has a tendency to consume everything in its path. The difference is that all-White spaces can often be inherently racist because Whiteness is reinforced as the norm against which everything else is measured.

What is important to understand here is that humanity's racial healing is not yet complete, and so the beloved community—that beautiful realm of God where racial identity is no longer an obstacle to relationship but rather something that is valued and celebrated—is not yet something we're ready for. So for now—at this point in our healing journey—White people need to spend time deconstructing our Whiteness while also understanding that BIPOC folk need to cultivate spaces that are safe for them. It's possible that our anti-racism efforts will result in a more diverse church because once we have tamed the power dynamic of Whiteness, BIPOC will feel safer. But if all we're trying to do is use the measure of how many BIPOC butts we have in our seats, we're not practicing anti-racism, but rather racist tokenism of Black and Brown bodies.

TIPS FOR SUCCESS

1. Create a journal specifically for this project.
2. Set aside time each week to engage this material regularly.
3. Leaders should go through the material individually (or, even better, with a trained coach) first. Only then should you engage your team, and when you do, you should have a solid plan of action for doing so.
4. Understand that while the time you spend engaging this book is important, much of your learning will come in the day-to-day practice, so keep your journal handy for those realizations when they come.
5. Prayer and meditation can be a powerful tool for transformation, and we encourage it throughout this process. Ask to be shown what you need to know. I believe this is a prayer God *always* answers.

QUESTIONS FOR REFLECTION BEFORE WE BEGIN

1. As you prepare to lead your organization to a place of true anti-racism, what fears come up for you? List them all honestly and without judgment. (You can't heal them without first acknowledging them.)
2. Do you notice any resistance to the introduction of this work? For example, how do you respond to the idea that anti-racism must include a divestment of power? What does this feel like in your body? Emotionally? It is important to be able to recognize resistance when it happens, because if you're not able to recognize it, you can't practice agency over it.
3. Does the way Bryana speaks of White guilt challenge your beliefs in any way? What feelings come up for you when you think of White guilt in this way?
4. How does your social location impact the way you see and understand racialized contexts?
5. What comes up for you when Josh invites you to love your *White* self? What about your identity can and do you love, and how is it related to your Whiteness?
6. Do the things you love about your Whiteness relate only to the power it offers, or are there other, more meaningful things that your White heritage can offer while also divesting itself of power?

PDF versions of the assessments found
throughout this book are available at
www.wjkbooks.com/WaitIsThisRacist
and may be printed for use by your teams
as you work through this book together.

1

Leadership

Ron was tall and rabidly funny, and on the day I first met him, he had his salt-and-pepper hair pulled into a short ponytail, a black beret with a matching turtleneck, and, of course, his trademark handlebar mustache, which he'd twirl with his fingers when he laughed, which was most of the time. He was my favorite boss ever for a number of reasons, not the least of which was the plethora of Yiddish proverbs he taught me, which I will forever and ever only hear in his voice. The one relevant to this chapter is this: *The fish stinks from the head.* Ron would say this often, with a shrug of the shoulders and his palms held up in supplication—a gesture that said, *You know what you know.*

It's one of the truest statements I've ever heard, and the good news is that good leadership can have just as much impact as its more olfactorily challenged counterpart. But when it comes to White people in positions of leadership over anti-racist spaces, things can get dicey, because our best of intentions can often do significant harm. A lot of times, that's because of plain old White hubris, encouraged by the belief that somewhere along the line, someone told White people we're the saviors of the world and we know how to fix everything.

We don't.

Let me tell you a story about White hubris and anti-racism. My friend Susan (not her real name) was a retail manager at a well-known food service chain that had a widely publicized incident in which police were called on some men who were, well, being *Black*. The response

15

was swift and public outcry rightfully harsh, so the chain closed its doors all over the country for some well-meaning anti-racism training. Susan told me a little about what actually happened at those training sessions. At twenty-two years old, and quite White herself, Susan was handed a manual and some brochures and was told to teach the material to employees who were mandated to be there. She never received any training in the material before she had to teach it. She felt ill-equipped to engage the material, much less instruct and lead others in the work, and she is fully aware that the "students" left the training unchanged.

But that's not all. The chain's leadership—and I know you'll be shocked to know it's mostly rich old White guys—thought it would be awesome to have its employees put little "race together" stickers on its products to, you know, encourage dialogue. With total strangers. About race.

Because that *always* goes well.

By ten o'clock that first morning, Susan had already encountered so many angry and abusive responses that she shoved the stickers under the counter and forgot the whole, really bad idea. (On a more entertaining note, however, Twitter did not disappoint with the ensuing hashtag amusement.) What happened to Susan was unfortunate—she was merely a pawn in a poorly thought-out leadership scheme, and the abuse she endured just for doing what she was told was unfair and really harmful. It was a long time before she was willing to even broach the topic again as a White person, which does nothing to help move the world toward anti-racism. But I'm also thinking of how many BIPOC were placed in horribly uncomfortable positions—whether they worked there or received a cup with the invitation to discuss their own oppression with the total stranger handing them their morning latte or breakfast wrap. It is the epitome of obtuse, White insensitivity, this idea that because racism doesn't cause us pain, the BIPOC community must love talking about it with us whenever we decide we're in the mood.

This was an obvious case of uninformed White leadership rushing to make well-intentioned but also really stupid gestures toward a "quick fix," without ever once considering impact. It is a perfect example of what "doing" anti-racism looks like without actually "being" anti-racist at your core. It represents a common phenomenon that occurs in White-led spaces: first, a dearth of proactive anti-racism results in a racist event, followed by knee-jerk and performative reactions by White leaders that don't really fix the problem, but make White people feel as though we've done something about the problem we caused in the first place. The result is more real harm—and this is why it's important that leaders do a deep dive into their own psyches to begin their own anti-racism work before they even start to think about leading others on this journey, whether individually or corporately.

This is not to say that as White leaders you won't make mistakes in your anti-racism work. You absolutely will. There will be messy moments, filled with complexity and nuance, and times when you feel doomed if you do and doomed if you don't. That all comes with the territory. Our goal, though, is to do as little harm as possible, and that can only happen if we are being existentially anti-racist. That means that every decision you make from now on gets considered through an anti-racist lens, first and foremost. As you begin to interrogate your work with anti-racism as a priority, you'll start noticing more of your potential mistakes *before you make them,* and more importantly, before you do harm. You can notice your inclinations and practice agency over them—and you might be surprised by where and when they show up.

WHITE DECISIONS

As White people, one of the important things we need to remember is that every thought, every perception, every decision we make is filtered through the lens of our Whiteness. This is not our fault, and we can't necessarily stop it from happening, but we *can* practice awareness and agency over it. Whiteness tends to both make assumptions and miss important information during the decision-making process. The story about Susan and the anti-bias training she was expected to implement is a perfect example of White leadership thinking they have enough information to handle a racial crisis. For example, leadership didn't think it was necessary to have trained personnel implement racial education for their staffs, nor did they consider the implications of having their retail employees handing out stickers encouraging racial dialogue with strangers. It's a perfect example of how Whiteness tends to leap before looking when it comes to race relations, rather than considering all the things it doesn't know—and should probably learn about—before taking action.

Key indicators that Whiteness is at play in your decision making might include aspects of individualism (rather than the collective), productivity and perfectionism (versus rest), peacekeeping and the status quo (instead of holy disruption for the sake of justice), and the prioritization of resources (especially financial) for the sake of the organization rather than the uplift of the marginalized. Another key indicator is an insistence on hierarchy and the hoarding of power. Shared power is a decidedly non-White form of leadership, and we tell ourselves a lot of myths about how it just can't work. It can, and it can work beautifully.

As we make decisions within our organization, it's important that we ask ourselves hard questions about the ways we might be perpetuating some of these aspects of Whiteness, because they don't just harm BIPOC—they harm all of us. For example, many of the churches I've worked with have staffs who are exhausted, overworked, and in some cases terrorized by leaders who insist they need to "work hard for God." This is a product of a misguided ethic that tells us our worth comes from our productivity rather than our inherent worth as human beings, and it harms White people and BIPOC alike. Still, the harm is exponential for Black and Brown folks because within White systems, marginalized communities such as BIPOC and women are often required to work even harder, be even better, have more letters after our names, and be even more perfect in order to survive the environments in which we work and live. If we instead become leaders who cultivate and prioritize rest for ourselves and our staffs, we are both resisting Whiteness and caring for our employees, and—call me crazy—that tends to yield pretty amazing results.

MITIGATING HARMFUL LEADERSHIP
(Bryana)

I was fresh out of the corporate world, ready and excited about this next chapter of life: helping organizations interrogate the ways in which they perpetuate racism within and beyond their walls. I wanted to bring a fresh perspective to race equity work by focusing most of my attention on the importance of understanding our racial history and encouraging individuals and organizations to invest in the "inner work" first. You know—the part many of us wish we could sneak past so we can get straight to the "doing." We seem to have this innate desire to "do" rather than to "be" because "being" would mean unlearning some hard pseudotruths about ourselves, our family, our friends, our country, our world, and our faith.

One of my first opportunities was to work with an organization that I formerly had been employed with, early in my career. They were holding their second annual Multicultural Summit, and they had asked one of my business partners to be a guest speaker. Given the increasing racial tension going on in the country, they, like many other organizations, were feeling overwhelmed, and they figured if they were hosting a summit with a multicultural theme, they better have someone talk about race. My business partner was White, and fairly new to her own "inner racial work." Her expertise was in gender equity and mentorship. So, naturally, they considered bringing me in as a cospeaker to address the race equity topic.

Then, just a few weeks before the summit, the organization decided they didn't want to invest in another speaker at the last minute, so they asked my White business partner to include some slides about race in her talk. No external speakers of color were paid to be on the panel. The one Black woman speaker was a current employee and, of course, she was not compensated for her time—the extra workload was assumed to be a "favor" since she was employed by the organization. To add insult to injury, they shared information on social media about my business partner, describing her as a "race equity expert" and highlighting the work she did under our shared business name.

This happens all the time. Well-meaning White people want to *do something,* and in their desperation, cause more harm to Black people than good. I had spent the majority of my career at this company and sat through hundreds of meetings in which I was the only Black person in the room. It was a company that did not have the race consciousness to recognize the potential risks of moving a young Black woman to rural parts of the country, where I called on primarily White customers who often verbally expressed their racist ideologies. Instead of choosing a speaker who had intimately experienced what it's like to be a Black person working there, they chose an ill-equipped White woman to present on race as if she were an expert. The topic of race was minimized to a sprinkle of slides, as an afterthought. I lost both an opportunity for income and a voice. The business name I shared with this speaker was used, with no compensation or attribution to me.

The unfortunate truth is that there likely wasn't a single White person involved who recognized the harmful impact this had, including my business partner. They carried on with their summit, chalked it up as a huge success, and moved on with their comfortable lives, feeling good about their efforts. I do not mean to imply that everything about this summit was harmful. I am confident there was a lot of great impact on certain individuals who were there, but the question I often ask myself is this: "If this work toward 'wokeness' involves harming BIPOC, is it really kin-dom work?"

YOUR TURN: DISCOVER YOUR RACIAL GENEALOGY (BRYANA)

How do White people gain the race consciousness needed to recognize when harm is being inflicted, even in the midst of good intentions? I want to share one concrete example of what this "inner work" can look like—what it looks like to "be" and not just "do."

This project is called "critical family history." It's not like the traditional genealogy projects with a focus on distant individual family members and their experiences (these projects are inherently easier for those of European descent due to the transatlantic slave trade and the erasure of Africans and African Americans in historical records). Christine Sleeter, an author, speaker, and activist, is credited for coining this term, which essentially refers to a "process of situating a family's history within an analysis of larger social relationships of power, particularly racism, colonization, patriarchy, and/or social class."[1] Sleeter explains that the combination of genealogy tools and historical research helps us understand how relations of power, in a given time and place, impact our families and the ways they participated in, constructed, experienced, and even resisted the culture and socialization of their time.

Our collective liberation as the body of Christ requires us to interrogate and lament and repent and seek truth, even when it's hard. After all, Jesus does teach us that the truth will set us free![2] As you and your church begin to delve into this work, here are a few questions you can consider about your personal genealogy (important work for anyone, but especially for a leader in anti-racism efforts as well as leadership of your organization) and your church's role in racial history.

ASSESSMENT 1.1: INTERROGATING OUR RACIAL GENEALOGY

1. When is the last time you looked at your individual family history through the lens of race? What about your church?
2. What was the role of your local church's lineage during the centuries of slavery? During the civil rights movement?
3. How has your church's history potentially perpetuated or resisted systemic racism?
4. What might an increased understanding of your church's critical family history do for your perspective as a church body in the role you play today in the work of anti-racism?
5. What might you need to lament—personally and corporately?
6. Of what might you need to repent?

THE DEEP MIDNIGHT OF THE WHITE SOUL

In a world where self-help books abound—and especially among the shiny-toothed, skinny-jeaned purveyors of health and wealth prosperity gospels and leadership-oriented Christianity—no leader gets up in the morning excited to guide their people into a deep midnight of the soul, filled with grief and lament.[3] Very few people want to go there themselves. But I am convinced that for White people to truly do this work, that's exactly where we need to be willing to go. To lead this work, that's where we need to be willing to lead others.

As a leadership coach and consultant, I've worked with pastors as they go through this journey. It often starts with a sense of resolute purpose, but as I continue to companion these well-meaning White people through the journey of education and racial awakening, a deep despair often takes hold. This is a perfectly normal and acceptable response to the horrific truth of systemic racism. Grief, anger, overwhelm, hopelessness, and shock are just some of the completely appropriate responses White people feel as we engage in the privilege of our own racial awakening. And make no mistake—getting to have a racial awakening (which means we got to have a long, luxurious racial nap) is indeed a privilege.

It's important to differentiate between **White grief** and **White tears**. "White tears" points to the problematic habit of White people centering ourselves and our feelings when we are confronted with our own racism. A perfect example of White tears occurred on the daytime television show *The Talk,* when Sheryl Underwood, a Black woman, confronted her White cohost Sharon Osbourne about her vocal support for a friend who had been accused of racist behavior.[4] During the conversation, Underwood was gentle in her questioning and consistently reassured Osbourne of their friendship, but Osbourne teared up at the thought that she might be perceived as racist, while also instructing Underwood that *she* was not allowed to cry—because Whiteness loves to police the ways in which Black people express their emotions. Next, Osbourne insisted with a toddler's sense of entitlement that Underwood teach her about her own participation in racist systems, demanding, "*Educate me!*" while simultaneously insisting that her actions were not racist. Osbourne claimed she felt as if she were being sent to the "electric chair" and even in her subsequent statements centered on the fact that she felt "blindsided" by the conversation and got defensive because of the "fear and horror" of being called a racist.

Comparing her perception of being called a racist to execution is harmful because she will absolutely survive being called a racist, but members of the BIPOC community are regularly executed by agents of the state for doing nothing at all. Demanding that Underwood educate her smacks of hubris—it is both a challenge, as if she doesn't believe Underwood will be able to deliver proof that racism is a thing, and deeply insensitive, in that it requires BIPOC to provide evidence of their own oppression to someone who won't believe it anyway. Finally, all of the attention was centered on Osbourne and her hurt feelings, rather than the actual point, which was the racial harm done by the friend she was vocally supporting. All of this is exactly what is meant by "White tears" and the centering of White people's emotions—primarily their fear of and offense at being associated with racism—which takes away from the learning and growth that can happen by actually talking about the impact of racist ideology.

This is different from White grief, which is a different emotion, expressed in a different way. White grief is a valid and appropriate response to the understanding that we have participated in harm. When I realize I have hurt someone I care about in deep and impactful ways, grief is absolutely a valid emotion for me to feel. Though my tendency might be to feel and express defensiveness, this is a sign of immaturity (and that's what results in White tears). When I am aware enough to instead examine my grief deeply, and then express it as true lament with a desire to initiate repentance and repair, I will express my grief differently, not centering my feelings but rather centering the harm I've done and asking how I might repair it.

Whether we are stuck in the destructive, defensive cycle of White tears or the deep lament of White grief, one thing is certain: none of these troublesome feelings get us off the hook. We still have to feel them. We have to sit with that gaping discomfort, that disharmonious truth in our soul that tells us we have been complicit in and have benefited from a system of oppression. We need to feel that grief in both our souls and our bodies, and let it touch us and teach us what we need to do next. Only when you have deeply engaged with yourself in this way can you begin the work of companioning others along the journey. And the work will be continual. You will always have to self-check. You will always be required to dance along your growth edge.

Let me be clear—I know that pastoral leadership is no light burden. Pastoring a congregation comes with a huge load to carry and it takes its toll emotionally. The self-awareness needed to confront your racial identity and care for others as they do the same is an additional labor, but it's a necessary one. It's important to practice self-care and, to Josh's point from the introduction, deep self-love through this journey, because ultimately, anti-racism work is about healing—healing ourselves, our racial divide, and the world.

REPRESENTATION IN LEADERSHIP

I once had the amazing opportunity to sit at the feet of Frances Hesselbein, the CEO of the Girl Scouts of America for many years and a world-renowned professional known for her leadership. She had to have been more than eighty years old at the time, and though she did teeter a bit at the podium, her voice was strong. She was fierce when she told us that if our organizations did not have multiple races represented on our leadership boards, we were perpetuating supremacist ideology and we needed to go home and address that issue before we did a single other thing. I agree with Ms. Hesselbein 100 percent. I also disagree with her vehemently. Because it's just not that simple, and as White leaders we have a whole lot of work to do before we start our next recruitment campaign.

Let me be clear. We absolutely need more BIPOC in positions of leadership, and that should be a matter of urgent concern. Not only is that just and right, it's also good for the world. New and different perspectives will bring innovation and diverse solutions, and this will be good for everyone. But one of the things Whiteness loves to do is check a box and call it a job well done. When filling leadership positions, this can and does result in the tokenization of Black and Brown people and the consumption of their time and energy in extremely unhealthy ways. That's why before we even think of hiring BIPOC to join our predominantly White staffs, we first need to do a few important things:

1. *Begin our own deconstruction.* As White people hoping to lead a diverse staff, we need to ensure that we have done (and are doing—because it's work that's never really complete) our own internal work to confront our Whiteness. We won't do this perfectly, but doing the work will at least lead us to ask the right questions and practice awareness and agency over our thoughts, speech, and behavior.

2. *Prepare to trust and submit to BIPOC leadership.* As part of our own internal work, we need to understand that often, Whiteness tends to think Whiteness knows best. A healthy White leader will check their tendency to second-guess Black and Brown leaders more frequently than White ones.

3. *Create a safe work environment for BIPOC, including an escalation path and safe mentors.* As Josh states in the sidebar, BIPOC leaders and staff face specific challenges in all White spaces that should be a matter of pastoral concern for White leaders. While you can't guarantee that your BIPOC staff will never experience a microaggression under your leadership, you can mitigate that likelihood by offering staff training and offering a clear **escalation path** and safe space for your BIPOC staff to address them when they do. (Keep reading for a more detailed discussion of this.)

4. *Engage in legacy planning that creates space for BIPOC leadership.* This may need to happen sooner than you think. I know more than one White leader who has stepped aside (or is planning to) because they know that their organization, and the communities in which they operate, would be better served by a Black leader. Being intentional about this means you are not only concerned with a more just present but also creating an anti-racist legacy.

BIPOC LEADERSHIP IN WHITE SPACES (JOSH)

If you're a BIPOC leader going through this book with your staff or team, it will be critical to prepare yourself for the journey. This process might dredge up past trauma or create feelings of resentment toward White colleagues on your team. You may feel strapped into the ups and downs of White guilt, shame, and anger as they process their own racial identity, and the pressure to comfort or affirm the White folks in the space—without much consideration for your own experiences, feelings, and needs—can feel like pulling a sharp turn on a ride at Six Flags. Whatever feelings or emotions arise, they are valid!

It will take some extra support to ensure your own sustainability through this process. I have found on my own journey that those who survive and thrive during the difficult work of racial equity are intentional about focusing on the following areas.

Find safe community. You will need to find spaces where your racial and ethnic identity is affirmed and celebrated and a community of care that is able to hold the fullness of who you are. While there is no one way to create this community, you can begin to assess what spaces you place yourself in now. Are they primarily White? Maybe you're the only ethnic minority in your book club, the coffee shop you frequent, or the yoga studio where you practice. It might be good to step out of these spaces if they can't affirm *all* of you.

You can redirect that time and energy into cultivating relationships in spaces with other BIPOC that affirm your racial and ethnic identity. This may seem scary and daunting at first, but these spaces exist and are worth seeking out. If you are not connected with this type of community already, it is a good practice to journal and reflect on how you arrived in predominantly White spaces.

Resist tokenism. Far too often marginalized communities—and especially BIPOC leaders—are asked to lead diversity and inclusion efforts simply because they are not White. This is tokenism, because not all of us are called to or interested in helping White folks work through their baggage—and that is OK! You are not required to lead or colead these efforts just because you are one of the few BIPOC leaders in your organization, and there is no shame if you are a BIPOC leader and uninterested in leading anti-racism efforts. Your organization may try to recruit you to lead these efforts because you're the only BIPOC they have access to, not because you're a passionate expert on the subject. You can exercise agency and set boundaries by saying no if helping facilitate anti-racism efforts is not an area of passion or experience for you.

Be compensated. Many who are passionate about anti-racism work and agree to participate end up experiencing an increased workload and job responsibilities. This generally happens without an increase in pay or support. Even if you are not part of leading these efforts, just your participation in the deconstruction of White pseudosupremacy is exhausting! If you are leading these efforts and it is beyond your regular job description, you deserve compensation for that; as Jesus said, "the laborer deserves to be paid."[5]

Churches that are serious about this work will recognize the added burden on you as a BIPOC and will find a way to offer more support. This does not have to be an increase in salary (although that is always nice). It can be extra time off or a mental health day added to your paid time off; it could be paying for the cost of counseling or therapy; it can even be financing educational experiences so you can be more effective in deconstructing White pseudosupremacy. Compensation should look like whatever is best for you! Be firm on your boundaries when leading any racial equity efforts if your needs can't be compensated in the process.

Work through your own baggage and trauma. This is where I plug therapy or counseling—and, for real, *please consider counseling.* No matter how old you are or how often you have deconstructed White pseudosupremacy, the burden remains immense. The process will dredge up old wounds or trauma, and finding a way to work through them will ensure your own sustainability as a leader. You may also come face-to-face with internalized racial narratives you did not even know you had! Processing those with a professional or in community is a crucial part of the healing process.

A Note on Recruiting BIPOC Staff

One of the most common myths I hear from White leaders is that as much as they might want to hire BIPOC, they just can't seem to find any quality candidates. I call this a myth because it is patently untrue that there is a dearth of talented BIPOC in the world, but I also understand that the frustration is real on the part of those who are seeking to hire them. The paradigm shift we need to make here involves not who is coming to us but rather where we are going to find our talent. If you are advertising your positions in the same old places, you'll get the same old results. Expanding your search for candidates to fill a position and spreading your net wider—and intentionally into BIPOC spaces—will help you attract a more diverse pool of potential employees.

ASSESSMENT 1.2: QUESTIONS FOR BIPOC LEADERS

1. What narratives and circumstances brought you to where you are now?
2. Who informed your understanding of leadership? Did those influences take into account your racial and cultural identity?
3. What are the risks for you in naming White pseudosupremacy in your church?
4. How do you understand the intersection of your racial identity with your other identities (sexuality, gender, physical/mental [dis]ability)? Do you experience any interlocking marginalization or privileges that come with these identities?

CREATING SAFE WORK ENVIRONMENTS FOR BIPOC STAFF

Work environments can be even more dangerous for staff members who embody marginalized identities than for leaders who do, because without even the symbolic power of a leadership position, they are subject to the additional stress of job insecurity. Couple this with the regular microaggressions they often have to endure on predominantly White staffs, and your efforts to diversify your staff may quite literally place the BIPOC you hire in harm's way. That doesn't mean you shouldn't hire them—which is often the response of dominance—but rather that before you hire them, you need to do the deep work of interrogating your own Whiteness; train staff in anti-racism, inherent bias, and microaggression awareness; and intentionally seek to create a space that allows BIPOC to not just survive, but thrive.

This may look different from what you expect. For example, it may mean investing in a trained BIPOC mentor who can be a safe means of support to help your BIPOC staff process the stresses of their job.

Despite your best efforts, it's possible that a staff member will experience racism on your watch, and it's important that there is a clearly communicated policy and path of escalation for when that occurs. That means everyone in your organization knows who to talk to and what to do if they feel unsafe—but that also means that you will have a plan for how you will respond to these issues. That's not to say every issue warrants the same response, but rather that you are ready and prepared to do the deep interrogation necessary to understand the racist event, care for the person who experienced it, and ensure it doesn't happen again.

The questions that follow are designed to help you become a leader who self-interrogates. There are no right or wrong answers; the questions are intended to spur you to deeper reflection and more powerful action. They are designed to expand your consciousness as a human being who leads. Engage the questions regularly, journal about them, discuss them with friends and colleagues. The ones that make you the most uncomfortable are the ones you need to sit with the longest, wrestle with the most. I invite you to pay attention and notice where you are most resistant, and always interrogate that feeling. Notice where your emotions appear in your body. Breathe through that and ask more questions of yourself. Practice deep curiosity about your own soul and lean into the genesis of your own imagination as we begin to create a new way of being White in the world without the construct of White pseudosupremacy.

CONCLUSION: THE PERFECTIONIST PRESSURES OF LEADING WHILE WHITE

Many White leaders go through their life and work never even noticing the ways in which their Whiteness impacts their leadership. Once you know, however, it's virtually impossible to unknow. That comes with a deep responsibility to do well, and here is where a key marker of **White culture** can become your greatest enemy: perfectionism.

If you let it, perfectionism will keep you from making the kinds of changes you need to make because you're afraid you're doing it wrong. And if we do make a mistake, the fallout is often so painful that we decide it's not worth it. The point to understand here is that, yep, you probably will do something wrong. Making racialized mistakes feels horrible, but they are exactly the kinds of learning experiences White people need to have. It doesn't help that as leaders, very often our mistakes are public. The key thing to remember is that the deciding factor is your response—and there are several typical responses that don't go well. Often, leaders try to erase their mistake and pretend it didn't happen. They respond with defensiveness rather than humility and a willingness to learn from their mistake. They keep talking when they really need to be quiet. It's important to think about how you will respond to these types of events when they occur, so that your response can be helpful, not harmful. Remember, mistakes handled well can lead us into the sort of deep introspection that results in true healing.

ASSESSMENT 1.3: QUESTIONS FOR WHITE LEADERS

Your Theology

1. Who are your theological influences and conversation partners? Are they all White? Are they all straight? Are they all cisgender? Are they all men?
2. Do you have a theology around Whiteness? What does Whiteness—or just the color white—symbolize to you?
3. What is your theology of darkness? Do you automatically associate darkness with evil? How might it be important to interrogate this theology when it comes to racial equity?
4. What narratives and circumstances brought you to where you are now, and how do they impact your own identity (racially and otherwise) and your assumptions about others? (This is a question Josh asked of BIPOC leaders, but I think it's an important question for White leaders to ask of themselves as well.) This can include stories that you hold about God, church, and family that impact your racial, sexual, gender, and cultural identities.

Your Identity

5. As Josh asks of those he works with, what aspects of your White heritage make you proud? You may have to dig deep

into your own cultural backgrounds to determine your own ancestral histories that make you who you are today. This is good and worthy work!

6. What are some indicators of your personal culture? Think about cultural markers: the holidays you celebrate and how you celebrate them; the foods you eat (and where they come from!); the music you listen to (and who creates it).

7. How is your own identity impacted by these cultural markers?

8. How has your religion and faith interacted with your Whiteness to make you who you are today? (Keep in mind that many of your answers to this question may not be immediately apparent, as they are constructed to be invisible to you. They may be uncomfortable when you do discover them.)

9. Have you done a racialized family genealogy, as Bryana suggested, for your own personal history? If so, what did you discover?

10. Think about the first time you remember being aware of race. What was the context? How did that contribute to your current racial awareness?

Your Opinions

11. When was the last time you read a point of view that was vastly different from your own?

12. Pay attention to the media you consume. Do you notice how members of the BIPOC community are portrayed, especially after incidents of violence against them? Is it positive, negative, or neutral? Is it true? Do you have the whole story? Do you need the whole story to remember that all human life is sacred?

13. Have you ever examined your opinions through a racial lens? Can you change your racial lens for a few moments to imagine a perspective that might be different from your White one? What happens when you do?

14. Have you curated a diverse social network and invested time and energy in real relationships with BIPOC, or is it filled with people who look and think like you? How many BIPOC voices are represented in your social media network?

Your Leadership

15. How has your Whiteness impacted your leadership? Where do you think your Whiteness limits your perspective? Can you even know?
16. When was the last time you thought you knew how to fix a problem? Did you have all the information? Did you consult people who were impacted? Did you know who was impacted? Did you consider impact when you implemented your solution?
17. What pressures do you feel as a White leader? Where do they come from?
18. What are the risks associated with you leading your church into an anti-racist stance? Think about personal relationships, finances, public relationships, and so on.

Your Team

19. Think about your team. How diverse is it? What hiring practices do you think contribute to your team's racial diversity (or lack thereof)? Be brutally honest. What are some steps you can take to create a more equitable hiring policy?
20. If you had to rate your team on its racial awareness, where would they fall? What steps might need to be taken to increase racial awakening?
21. Are there BIPOC on your team? What do you think their experience is like?

Your Organization

22. When you think about the fact that you or your organization may be embodying racist ideology, what is your emotional response? Where does that show up in your body? What does that feel like?
23. Has your organization done a racial genealogy? If so, what did you discover? If not, how might you begin that process?
24. When you imagine your organization living into a fully anti-racist identity, how is it different from how it is today?

2

Preaching and Liturgy

The preacher was young—an up-and-coming leader, son of the lead pastor, and someone I liked immensely. He was crazy smart and funny, bearded and appropriately hip, and I always enjoyed our conversations as well as the sermons he delivered fairly regularly at my church. But one day was very different—one day, the power of the pulpit sent a clear message about the value of my humanity, and it's a moment I'll never forget.

It started off OK. He began telling the story of a renowned poker player—a man famous for his cigar-smoking debauchery almost more than his ability to play cards. It was obvious that the speaker was using this man as an example of How Not to Be, and his description was entertaining and engrossing until he got to one important detail: one of the things this man was famous for was paying two bikini-clad women to sit next to him and stroke his beard.

That's it. Just sit there. In bikinis. Petting his facial hair.

I confess that at this point, I was still enthralled and waited not-so-patiently for this passionate young preacher to continue his train of thought about how this was simply not an awesome way to be in the world. I was excited that finally we might hear a message from the pulpit—even if it was just a small aside in a larger sermon about something else entirely—that women are not mere ornaments intended to hang on the arms of men, and that we should not be objectified as simply the underdressed complements of men's bodies. I confess that

I was hanging on every word, waiting for the affirmation of a woman's full humanity. Of *my* full humanity.

But that's not what happened.

What happened instead left me reeling and unable to pay attention to the rest of the sermon, because what followed absolutely did *not* affirm my humanity as a woman. Instead, he struck a pose, touched his own beard, and said, "And I thought, I could get used to that. That would be pretty cool, to have two beautiful women in bikinis follow me around and stroke my beard."

I felt a sickness in my belly and an anger burning in my throat as the majority of the audience around me laughed. I felt my jaw fall open—I'm not sure if it was shock, anger, or disappointment that made it go slack, but I know I felt all of those emotions. I was heartbroken, too. In one of those hyperfocused moments that happen when emotions run high, I glanced at the woman sitting next to me. I didn't know her, and she did not look at me. But her body language told me everything I needed to know—her hands were gripped tightly in her lap; her body was straight and rigid; her jaw was clenched. I remember the straight slash of her red lipstick against her dark skin, the way the side of her cheek twitched with the same tension I felt. She was not laughing with the rest of the audience. She felt it, too. A little bit of our being, a little bit of our humanity had just been stolen away. Our objectification had just been reinforced and institutionalized by the power of the pulpit. And it happened in the guise of a joke.

PREACHING AS POWER

The power of the pulpit is an important aspect in any system of dominance. We are going to examine together two parts of the church service: the pulpit and its messages, and our liturgies and what they communicate. But before we examine what happens in these two areas, let's look at *why* they are so incredibly powerful. To do this, we need to understand the psychology of power, the way it works, and how to divest it.

First, let's work with some definitions and distinctions. For our purposes here, let's define *power* as the positional ability to make something happen. *Influence,* on the other hand, is the ability to sway opinion through relationship, perception, or position. For example, as the lead pastor, you may hold power to make final decisions over budgetary items, but there may be key members of your congregation who hold sway over what you ultimately decide. Your positional power may be mitigated by their influence over public opinion. Key to the impact of influence are the ideas of relationship, perception, and position, especially when it comes to our discussion of the power of the pulpit. These three dynamics often operate invisibly (as most power dynamics do), but that doesn't make them less potent. Those who bear the title of pastor or preacher often navigate all of them: you are in relationship with your congregants (often as spiritual guide and trusted counselor); you are perceived as good, godly, and a spiritual "expert"; and you hold a position of authority and power (the ability to make things happen).

Within physical space, your messages are often delivered from an elevated platform that places you not just in front of people but also above them. That means every time you step into the pulpit, your words are given an extra weight of authority in the minds of the people who are listening, even if they don't realize it's happening. It's important, however, to understand this is contextual and may change based on your particular embodiment. For example, if you're a White, cis-hetero man, you may choose to preach from the floor rather than an elevated pulpit as a symbol of humility and a desire to resist your power. On the other hand, a dear friend of mine who is both a woman and a pastor is adamant about taking up her space in the ornate and elevated pulpit in her church's historic building, simply because she wants people to get used to seeing female authority in that sacred place of power. Both of these are excellent examples of how our embodiment can be a tool for resistance simply by considering who we are and where we place our bodies in proximity to power. Neither of them, however, address how accessible that elevated pulpit may be to everyone. For example, do stairs create an obstacle for some people, keeping their voices silenced? Do you have a sign language interpreter for people who are hearing impaired?

In some religious contexts (and in the subconscious minds of the people who come from them), you may even be a direct representative of God. That's why it's so important to be both aware of and highly intentional about what symbols, images, and messages are conveyed by the pulpit. Because here's the thing: I don't think that young pastor would actually be cool with objectifying women. The man I imagine him to be is someone who would never want to do that. But now? I can't be so sure. And even worse, by telling that joke from the power of the pulpit, he just gave all the men in that room permission to objectify and dehumanize women, because what's acceptable for the pastor must be acceptable for all men (and also the women with internalized misogyny). Not only that, the message that women received was that we are only as good as our ability to wear a bikini and stroke a man's whiskers.

I trust that most of you are not struggling over whether or not to include stories of bikini-clad women in your sermons (and if you are, consider yourself forewarned). But that doesn't mean you've cleared the minefield, or even done the work. I was recently working with a church's anti-racism task force, and one of the members showed great resistance to the idea that anti-racism can show up in every sermon. "Not every sermon can possibly be about anti-racism!" he exclaimed, heatedly. But you can preach an anti-racist sermon that isn't about race at all. What we are attempting to do here is to replace our White lens with an anti-racist one. That means that when we preach Scripture, we are interpreting it through a liberative bent. When we use examples and stories, we wisely choose topics that demonstrate anti-racism. And when we encounter problematic Scriptures that seem to prop up dominance, we acknowledge that, we interrogate and struggle with it, and we find a way to liberation through it. So not every sermon has to be about race, but every sermon can absolutely be anti-racist. I will even take this point further and say that if your anti-racist sermons are only showing up during your Black History Month sermon series, you're not actually being anti-racist at all.

Those of us who write sermons need to be vigilant about the imagery we use in our preaching—even that which might feel comfortable and familiar. For example, I've had more than one argument with my fellow White preachers about the ways in which we use "darkness" in our dialogue. I know the Bible uses it, and I'm here to remind us that many of us have decided other parts of the Bible are problematic, so we'll be fine if we tackle this one, too. And, like many (but not all) other problematic areas of Scripture, it has more to do with interpretation than with the actual words. For our purposes here, I think it's important to resist the metaphor that equates darkness with anything construed as evil, bad, witchy, or demonic.

Other common metaphors that show up in our preaching often have more to do with warring armies and empirical powers than with the marginalized and oppressed. If we are encouraging our congregants to participate in "kingdom work," practice religious warfare, or exist under "reigns," we are speaking the language of empire, not of Holy

Spirit. Even if we are encouraging the underdog to be victorious, the imagery of the "victor," of reigns and fortresses and armies, is all merely two sides of the same denarius. I challenge us all to lean into our imaginative edges to envision a realm of God that is more banquet table than bulwark, more beloved community than kingdoms and principalities.

Similarly, the repetition of liturgy makes it a powerful force in the minds and hearts of the people who participate in worship, so it's important that we are being intentional about the imagery and messages we are communicating within it. People very rarely interrogate their own embedded beliefs, but when we do, we're often surprised to discover that we have no idea where they came from. The truth is that narrative is all around us, developing our belief system, and you can be sure that if someone is attending church regularly, the imagery and messaging to which they are subjected on a weekly basis is going to impact their worldview, whether they know it or not.

Like most ritual, Christian liturgy serves a few purposes: (1) it sustains a memory or keeps events alive; (2) it creates a social fellowship around the memorialized event; and (3) it offers people an opportunity to rededicate themselves to the event.[1] That means that when we gather to perform liturgy (unlike when we gather for social reasons or to celebrate a holiday or an event like a graduation) we are gathering to remember the Jesus story and all that goes with it. That includes imperial oppression, marginalization of populations, state-sanctioned lynchings, and other injustices pertaining to power and the oppressed. Sustaining memory is important, and if we only perform the ritual for ritual's sake, we are missing an important aspect of doing church that is highly applicable to our purposes here.

Liturgy also represents a formalized experience of the divine done in community, and as such, it becomes a social contract of its own kind—it is the collective agreement of belief in the message that is being conveyed. If that message aligns with empire rather than the oppressed, with dominance rather than the meek, with Whiteness and not with our Black and Brown siblings, then our liturgies are racist and perpetuating supremacy culture. Liturgy is about shared story—and if some people are left out of that story because of misguided norms, centered dominance, and pseudosupremacy, we're doing it wrong. The good news is that our liturgies also allow us an opportunity to remember the fractures of our societal sins, because the sins that killed Jesus are the same sins that killed George Floyd, Ahmaud Arbery, Philando Castile, and so many others. Our liturgies offer us an important chance to remember the souls lost to the injustice of oppressive systems and therefore to *re-member* ourselves to each other in community.

THE EMBODIED PULPIT

Now that we understand a little about why these two parts of doing church—sermons and liturgy—are so powerful, it's time to examine the way that Whiteness, pseudosupremacy, and racism can weave through them and perpetuate dominance rather than dismantle it. I opened the chapter with a story that demonstrates embedded patriarchy, misogyny, and sexism in a sermon, presented as merely a joke, and I've pointed out why that's troublesome. I can honestly tell you that the man who made that joke is a genuinely kind and caring person. Though his identity as a cis-hetero White man may make it impossible for him to fully understand the damage his joke did, I genuinely do not think he intended to do any damage at all. I know you do not intend to do damage to any marginalized group in your preaching, either. As White leaders who regularly speak from the power of the pulpit, one of the greatest strides we can make toward being anti-racist is to admit that we don't know what we don't know, because this acknowledgment leads us to ask deeper questions of ourselves, to be more careful and calculated with our choices. When it comes to being anti-racist, this is a very good thing.

As I study systems of dominance like White pseudosupremacy, I become more and more convinced that the leadership of the future must be from the collective. You may be the voice coming from the pulpit, but that doesn't mean that you have to simply regurgitate White theology over and over again. The first step toward collective leadership is to not just read BIPOC voices, but to allow yourself and your sermons to be infused with and influenced by them. Ideally, your congregation will know exactly who you're reading and how they've influenced you, too. I am convinced that it's very difficult, for example, to read Womanist theology and not come away with a more expansive view of God and the Divine at work on earth. If more congregations were exposed to the ethos of Womanism, the world would be a much better place. The point here is that sermons that are expanded beyond the same old White theologies to include feminist, Womanist, Mujerista, and liberation theologies will impact us spiritually and change us behaviorally, and when those theologies begin to infuse your sermons, they can help spur your congregation on to a more deeply held anti-racist stance.

It's a great start to be influenced by these other theologies, but it's even better to offer your pulpit to be occupied by bodies that are different from yours. I am purposeful in referring to embodiment here, because the more your White congregation experiences different types of bodies doing theology, the closer we all get to the realm of God. If we say we want to create a more just world but we are unwilling to even begin by divesting ourselves of the power of the pulpit, then we're simply not going to get very far.

Very often in the churches I've worked with there is an "inner circle"—a well-fortressed center of power that consists of a few core leaders who call all the shots. Proximity to this inner circle equates to influence—the closer you are to the center, the more likely you are to get what you want. For supremacy culture to divest itself of power, we need to be thinking of ways in which we who hold power can actively use it to pull those who hover on the margins into the center, so that the center circle of power becomes a sort of pooling pond through which many voices flow. The pulpit—that most visible symbol of leadership in the church—must belong to the collective, and the fullness of the collective must be represented.

Divesting Whiteness of its power means that we examine the way Whiteness operates in our sermons and in the embodied pulpit. Whose voice gets to ring from that privileged podium? Whose body gets to take up space there?

WHO GETS TO HOLD THE MIC

(Josh)

How a church uses its pulpit is often evidence of its capacity to practice anti-racism. Many of the churches I work with are unwilling to disrupt the power dynamic of who preaches. As you move through your journey, this is a rich space to interrogate and identify what is at stake to change and disrupt who gets to hold the mic and share a sermon. What is at stake is not just what is preached, but *who* gets to communicate narratives around patriarchy, ableism, colonialism, and White pseudosupremacy.

There is an urgent need to decenter Whiteness in the pulpit, and an excellent place to start is to ensure that your sources express a diverse range of experiences and identities. Commentaries, scholars, and writers that inform your sermons should be conscious of power dynamics and cultural nuances that shape the biblical text. This can spell the difference between preaching stories that reinforce harm and dehumanization or preaching liberation and empowerment. The extensive work of BIPOC biblical scholars and writers brings a texture to the biblical narrative that White readers might otherwise miss. Incorporating these voices can help lead to a more expansive understanding of the text while disrupting harmful or problematic interpretations and sermons.

I have heard too many sermons on Abraham that skate right past the fact that he accumulated massive wealth by pimping out his wife and taking agency over her body to save his own life. (See Gen. 12:10–20 and 20:1–18 if you think I am kidding.) What would happen if we centered the narrative around Sarah or, better yet, Hagar? They are both survivors, and both had their bodies plundered by Abraham. What does it say about the God we serve if we can only celebrate men like Abraham and not wrestle with the complexity and pain his narrative brought to those around him? Telling the whole story could be healing and liberating to those in your congregation who are sexual assault survivors themselves!

Intentionally seeking out the women in the texts that are preached on can help decenter Whiteness in your sermons too. They are almost always present in the text but have been erased and marginalized by pastors, biblical scholars, theologians, and sometimes the authors of the original text. If women aren't active characters in the text, invite your congregation to ask why and consider their experience in the story.

One of the most frequent objections I hear from pastors on this journey is to the idea of "stepping back" from the pulpit. In all the churches I consult or coach, I always ask before we get started in any meaningful work: "In the last two years, how many times has a BIPOC woman preached here?" This question seems shocking; most can name only three or four times at most—out of more than a hundred Sundays!—when a BIPOC shared a sermon from a pulpit. Quoting or citing BIPOC theologians and preachers is a good move, but getting out of their way so they can lift their own voices from the pulpit is a critical step, and I am not just talking about a sermon on race. One of the best ways you can shepherd your church is to sit your behind down and model what it looks like to listen well to your BIPOC family in God.

A pastor I was coaching was eager to start this process. He bought all the big-time commentaries by BIPOC and was ready to begin quoting James Cone and Gustavo Gutiérrez as often as possible. But when asked how many BIPOC voices he would make space for at the pulpit, he faltered. He was not comfortable inviting new folks to preach beyond a small cohort of pastors in his network. His network looked and preached just like him and could only reinforce the norms he sought to disrupt. He knew they could not be helpful in the disruption of White pseudo-supremacy in the congregation but was hesitant to take the initiative in inviting BIPOC speakers outside of said curated network.

This is a place where many White pastors get caught up. The desire to be the person who preaches and teaches anti-racism is often greater than their willingness to make space for BIPOC to be in a position of power they usually occupy. The pastors I work with present all sorts of reasons why they cannot relinquish the pulpit more than the few Sundays a year that they don't preach—everything from theological purity tests to elder board preaching requirements placed on the pastor. All of these reasons ensure making space for BIPOC to preach and teach (not just on the Sunday preceding Martin Luther King Day) is not easy or even possible.

Decentering Whiteness in your pulpit also means disrupting the system that cements the White voice as the dominant one in the congregation's life. These are holy disruptions that make space for the Divine to manifest in surprising and beautiful ways! So, read and study diversely, and make room in the pulpit for the voices on the margins of our society. Compensate them well and ensure their presence is not only a one-off sermon about race.

LITURGICAL IMPACT

(Bryana)

> I do not remember how or when, but I know that by the time I had learned that God is love, that Jesus is His Son, that all men are brothers with a common Father, I also knew that I was better than a Negro.
> —Lillian Smith[2]

Though Lillian Smith, a White activist and writer, wrote this in 1949, the present-day experience for a White churchgoer (or a BIPOC growing up in a predominantly White church) from adolescence into adulthood is likely not much different. Why is that? What messages about "Whiteness" and "anti-Blackness" are we sending from the pulpit and in our church communities in mostly implicit ways? Now that you have a baseline understanding of power and influence, let's further explore how implicit messages are given and received in our liturgical spaces and experiences from a sensory perspective: sight (imagery) and sound (language).

Imagery

As I reflect on my childhood experiences with imagery in the church, I quickly flash back to my teenage years. I'm about thirteen years old, and like every Sunday before this Sunday, I'm out of bed early and already picking out my Sunday outfit. Before I finish getting ready, I'm in Mom and Dad's room, shaking their bed and encouraging them to get up and ready before we are late to church. I loved church. Sunday mornings (and afternoon youth group) were my favorite parts of the weekend. As we roll into church, a few minutes late as always, we pass through the narthex adorned with images from Bible stories hung on the walls. White Jesus. White Mary. White angels. White. White. White.

We sneak into the back of the sanctuary and find our place about halfway up the aisle (where we always sat), passing warm White faces of our church family as we usher ourselves into the pew and find the spot in the hymnal to follow along to the song that is playing. I loved my church family. They are the reason I'm a believer. They encouraged me, and loved me, and challenged me throughout my faith journey. But none of them looked like me. My father was the only Black person in our entire congregation. All of my pastors were White men, except one: Pastor Deb, a White woman. I vividly remember that her arrival shook things up for our little church. Some people even disappeared from Sunday service after Pastor Deb arrived, never to return to our church again.

In Sunday school, my teachers were White. The books we read had White Bible characters. The dolls in the church nursery were White. My whole faith upbringing was, well, White! The pastors and church leaders never had to talk to me about racial dynamics for me to get a pretty clear, yet "hidden" message about my Blackness—my father's Blackness. And also about Whiteness.

Race is deeply embedded in the structure of Christianity, and it was used to justify the beginnings of colonialism and slavery. Colonizers justified theft of land, genocide, and the enslavement of human beings for profit by animalizing Black folk and dehumanizing Indigenous peoples. In 1448, the first slave dungeon was built in Elmina (West

Africa), where millions of Africans were forced onto ships headed to the Americas.[3] For 400 years, Europeans would rape, torture, mutilate, murder, and capture Africans in this location. Conveniently for the Europeans, there was a Christian (Catholic) church right in the center of the slave dungeon.[4] One minute, they were worshiping at church, and the next, they would go right above the church to the auction hall, to sell the Africans they enslaved. As Black Liberation theologian James Cone poignantly points out, "The God of the people who were riding on the decks of the slave ship is not the God of the people who were riding underneath the decks as slaves in chains. The God you're praying to bless slavery is not the same God of those praying, 'get us out of slavery.'"[5]

Do not underestimate the power of images and representation in your church buildings. Even if the pews are filled with kind and faithful White people, BIPOC representation in your paintings, stories, nursery books and dolls, and even music (that's for a later chapter) is so important.

Language

Deeply intertwined with imagery is language. Language is powerful. In the church, theology is often expressed in the language that is used. From a liturgical context, this may require us to think about how we phrase the execution (or lynching) of Jesus Christ. For example, rather than saying, "Jesus died on the cross," let's get real with the historical truth that Jesus was executed (lynched) by the state. I am not a theologian, nor an expert on liberation theology; however, I am fascinated by the history of the creation of this theology, founded by Gustavo Gutiérrez, a Roman Catholic theologian and Dominican priest.[6] Black Liberation theology reads the Bible through the experience of those who suffered. After all, the Bible was written by the oppressed! When we read the Bible from the margins, this requires us to ask questions such as "Who do we identify with most in this story?" and "Whose stories are not being told?" For example, when you tell the exodus story, do you question why Miriam (Moses' sister, who saves his life) isn't even named in this story? Do you identify with the oppressed Hebrews or with the Egyptians, who hold the power and privilege in this situation?

As James Cone explained in a speech at Princeton Theological Seminary in 1980,

Liberation theology has been created by people who consciously seek to speak to and for the victims of economic and political injustice as represented in racism, classism and sexism. The advocates of this new theology are intolerant of any perspective of Christianity that fails to relate the Gospel of Jesus to the economic and social conditions of people. . . . Because I am a black North American theologian, whose political and religious consciousness has been shaped in and by black peoples' historical fight for justice, I agree with my theological colleagues in Asia, Africa, and Latin America, who contend that the Gospel cannot be separated from the concrete struggles of freedom among the oppressed of the land.[7]

Just as we need to not underestimate the power of imagery, we must also not underestimate the power of language. As you continue on this journey, find ways to leverage your power and influence to call attention to the words, stories, and perspectives of those who are oppressed—both in the Scriptures and in your own society.

DOMINANCE IN LITURGICAL PRACTICES

Because ritual and rite are such powerful ways to embed theology and ideology into our brains, it's important to be intentional with the imagery and messaging contained in them. Do the Scriptures we highlight support empire or the marginalized? If you incorporate a modern element in your liturgy, such as poetry, ask yourself who wrote it, and what it actually says about God, Whiteness, or BIPOC. (Remember, it can say a lot without ever mentioning Whiteness or Blackness.) Do your calls to worship truly invite all or are they somehow exclusionary? Does your confession include the acknowledgment of corporate sin, of the sins of the church as an organization, of Whiteness? These are all opportunities to resist White pseudosupremacy and to practice liturgy as a true remembrance.

I could probably write an entire chapter about each liturgical element, but let's instead do a deep dive into the Eucharist as an example of how you might examine each part of your church's ritual. In their book *A Body Broken, A Body Betrayed: Race, Memory and Eucharist in White-Dominant Churches,* authors Marcia W. Mount Shoop and Mary McClintock Fulkerson say, "A dominant contemporary White narrative is that of the church as a welcoming, colorblind community that gathers at the Table regularly to be reconciled with God."[8] The church is choosing, then, to not see the glorious colors that humans come in, because color blindness is not really color-blind at all—it merely centers Whiteness as the norm and claims to see everyone as White, as long as they don't act too Black or Brown. The authors go on to say, "If Christ's presence [at the Table] has to do with bodies—his, of course, and ours as the 'Body of Christ'—then the bodies at the Table matter."[9]

According to Shoop and Fulkerson, the Eucharist is supposed to be about social trauma (the execution of Jesus by the state, the ongoing oppression of the marginalized by empire) and relational betrayal (Judas's turning, the denial of Jesus by multiple disciples), but the practice has been sanitized and **White-washed** by dominant identities into a mild practice of wafers and wine. Often, that practice is carried out with other bodies that look an awful lot like our own, and if they don't, we pretend they do. We are missing a vast and wide opportunity to both remember the social trauma of our own day, to commemorate the bodies broken by the state on our own streets, and to re-member the bodies betrayed by the disfigurement of our own White souls. This re-membering—this coming back together of that which had been dismembered and torn apart—is a necessary step in creating the kin-dom of God and the beloved community. What could be a meaningful ritual of memory and re-membering, of communion and the collective, has instead become another way to conceal and deny White participation in the dehumanization of Black and Brown people. Because this liturgical practice does nothing to represent the pain of our racialized horrors, it also does nothing to heal them.

In a church that wants to be truly anti-racist, Eucharist can demonstrate both our distortion and our redemption, say the authors. The beauty and tragedy of the Last Supper is that it is not just the story of a leader's last meal with his friends, but it also speaks to relational rupture and interpersonal betrayal. There is deep sadness and grief in knowing that Jesus is the victim of a literal conspiracy against him, and also that one of his closest friends participated in his betrayal. It is so easy to flatten the emotion against the text of the page, but the passion of these emotions is all too real if you've ever felt this type of relational rupture, the brokenheartedness that occurs amid deep betrayal. The problem is the love doesn't go away, and that often only makes it all feel worse. Jesus embodied this at the Last Supper, but we have lost our passion to remember the broken communities that are often residing just outside our church doors. Jesus' love for Judas did not disappear at the moment of his betrayal. It just made it all the more painful.

It is important for White-dominant churches to understand that in this telling of the Communion narrative, we are Judas, not Jesus.

What is a Judas to do, then?

Perhaps it is time to respond not with sanitized rites that keep truth comfortably distant but rather to bring our grief and lament to the table of brokenness so that we may be re-membered with those communities from whom we have torn ourselves. Maybe we can do the hard work of looking, and finally see the gory truth of the crucifixion. Rather than looking away, we can *look and see* the red stain on Philando Castile's T-shirt and remember him when we drink the wine. We can *look and see* the knee on George Floyd's neck, and feel our breath fill our own lungs after we swallow the bread. Whiteness loves to look away from these things, to make them neat and orderly. But lynchings are violent and the crucifixion, grisly. This was true when it happened to Jesus, and it's true today when it happens so often on our streets. Eucharist gives us a chance to remember, and in doing so, we take a step closer to being re-membered.

Only then, once we have remembered and been re-membered, might we move on to a new way of being. John's Gospel tells a different account of Jesus' last night with the disciples, and it represents embodied servanthood in the washing of feet as an act of radical love. Shoop and Fulkerson remind us that the Last Supper was itself a commemoration of Passover, re-membering that sacred story of liberation.[10] In other words, as we practice the liturgy that helps us remember Jesus' last moments with his friends, we need to intend to awaken the collective memory of radical love and God's liberative motivations as well as societal violence, betrayal, and relational rupture.

A beautiful way to do this is to take Communion outside the church, rather than keeping it an inside job. Shoop and Fulkerson tell a beautiful story of a collective who took Communion to a protest to break bread in public as a way to re-member the hungry and the marginalized. In their prayer, they commemorated not just the Christian tradition of God blessing two fish and five loaves and feeding five thousand bellies, but also how Muslims cannot celebrate the Eid (feast) until each person has offered charity to the hungry. They re-membered the African proverb that speaks of knowing another's pain by breaking bread together.

They carried their Communion liturgy through the state capitol building, praying, singing, and sharing bread, this diverse group of people from all races, socioeconomic backgrounds, and faith traditions. This act of collective Communion is decidedly anti-empire and anti-racist, and it represents a new way to think about an old tradition that resists supremacy culture.

As you begin to work through the following questions around preaching and liturgy, keep in mind the constructs of power and influence, imagery and narrative, embedded beliefs and institutionalized messaging. Think about how these are in partnership with Whiteness and other dominant identities, and how you might divest that power to the collective. (Remember that we will be looking at music in the next chapter.)

ASSESSMENT 2.1: PREACHING

1. From where do you preach? Where is your location relative to the people to whom you are preaching? Does your preaching location subvert or perpetuate dominance?
2. Who preaches? Do you offer the pulpit to embodied voices different from yours?
3. Is the pulpit literally and physically accessible to all (all races, all body types, all genders, etc.)?
4. When you preach, who is influencing your sermon? Do you consult Womanist, Black Liberation, or Mujerista theologies, for instance? Do you acknowledge or allow Indigenous practices to inform your sermons?
5. What symbols of empire are included in your preaching? Do you speak of kingdoms, reigns, and warfare imagery in a positive way? How might that affect or impact those members of your congregation who are disempowered and subject to oppression (women, members of the BIPOC and LGBTQ communities, the differently abled, the very old, the very young, or those living below the poverty line, for example)?
6. When you interpret biblical stories, do you always align yourself (or your congregation) with the "good guys"? Are you always Moses, never Pharaoh? How do the narratives change when you become Pharaoh, Judas, or Pontius Pilate, for example?

ASSESSMENT 2.2: LITURGY

1. Reviewing your liturgical elements, do you find any alignment with empire in them? How could they better resist empire?
2. How are the marginalized represented in your liturgies, if at all? Are there deeper, more meaningful ways in which their perspective can be not just included, but centered?
3. Who performs your liturgies? Are they exclusively performed only by certain people with power? If so, why? Is this church polity? How can that exclusivity be resisted?
4. Do your liturgical practices re-member relational, racial, and societal rupture? If not, what changes can you make so that your practice is less White-washed and sanitized?
5. Do you teach your congregation how to approach and interpret the Bible? If so, do you approach it with a liberative bent?
6. What does it mean to understand the Bible from the perspective of those in the margins? What would that look like?
7. As a White pastor or leader in a church, in what ways have you internalized the norms of Whiteness, and how does that specifically impact the way you interpret Scripture and craft liturgy?
8. Who are the gatekeepers who might be preventing the pulpit from being more diverse and inclusive? How are you engaging these gatekeepers to ensure marginalized voices are heard during Sunday sermons?
9. Take an audit of the preaching and teaching resources used at your church. How many of these resources come from BIPOC, queer, or differently abled voices?
10. If you're a church leader or staff member, how are you modeling listening to BIPOC voices for your congregation? Do you name the BIPOC sources you quote? How do you include BIPOC voices in your anti-racism journey?

3

Music

There is nothing more fun than a good song, and my iTunes runs the gamut from *Hamilton* and *Wicked* to Kendrick Lamar, from John Denver to The Pogues, Sex Pistols to Concrete Blonde, Everclear to Abba. There's some funk on there and a little bit of disco (but not too much) and of course a full library of Indigo Girls. There is a ton of alternative music from back when alternative actually was alternative, with its own radio station and everything. But one song in particular has taught me a disturbing lesson about the power of music to invisibly propagate that which I stand against, all while I happily bop my head along to the beat: "Walk This Way" by Aerosmith.

I love this song, and I hate that I love this song.

I live a busy life and I'm often on autopilot, so I don't always make it a habit to look up the lyrics to songs unless they really grab me. I don't remember why I looked up these particular lyrics, but I can tell you that once I did, I was horrified. Hidden beneath that badass beat and that really hot guitar riff are lyrics that serve up a heaping dose of hypersexualized young girls, the commodification of the female body traded for sexual favors, and a steaming pile of pedophilia on the side. It's ruined the song for me. What's worse, its normalization of this horrific sexual ethic was disturbingly driven home when Aerosmith joined Jimmy Fallon and the Roots to play the song on a *Tonight Show* segment called "Classroom Instruments," in which the song was played on musical toys for children. It's a great segment—it's fun, the song is as "good" as ever, and the video (which you can easily access with Google) is super entertaining. But when you're aware of the song's meaning and everything that it stands for, it's also deeply disturbing in multiple ways.

The thing is that once you know, you can't *unknow*.

On the other hand, I've also seen music used as a beautiful act of resistance and solidarity. I remember staring at my screen, watching a report from the 2019 special session of the General Conference of the United Methodist Church, at which a controversial vote was taken regarding LGBTQ+ inclusion. I was brought to tears as I watched a group of clergy, shut out of the proceedings and forced to stand in the lobby, gather and sing "For Everyone Born, A Place at the Table." I was encouraged by their solidarity as they sang the powerful words, "God will delight when we are creators of justice."[1] Another powerful musical moment was when, during the 2019 protests in Hong Kong, a crowd of demonstrators sang the well-known anthem from *Les Misérables*, "Do You Hear the People Sing?," as a way to galvanize the participants while also funneling their energy into peaceful action.[2]

Music can be a powerful motivator, an inspirational educator, and a tool for propaganda. Music is woven into the tapestry of our lives, creating soundtracks to important life events and background grooves to our most meaningful moments. It is deeply connected with emotion and identity, and that's why it's so easy to be passive about the music in our lives. It's been there forever, it's comforting, it's in the background, and we often don't even notice the full impact it has on us. That's what makes it important enough to be really intentional about—so much so that it gets a whole chapter of this book all to itself.

If we're not careful, our passivity around maintaining the musical status quo means that our cherished hymns might be infiltrating our psyches with supremacy culture, nationalist propaganda, and the mind-set of the colonizer rather than an alignment with the meek and the marginalized. Because they are the songs of an institution, this is important. It's one thing if we're humming a tune in our cars; it's an entirely different thing if we are collectively singing as a corporate body that represents an alleged "right relationship" with God.

THE POWER OF MUSIC: EMOTION, IDENTITY, AND ACTION

What is it about music that makes it so powerful? Kathleen M. Higgins, a professor of philosophy at the University of Texas who studies aesthetics and the philosophy of emotion, claims that music creates an intimate solidarity. Because the vibrations of sound actually enter our bodies, aligning them with the music, a corporate musical experience also aligns us with *each other*. Though it may happen only subliminally, we are entrained when we listen to music to adopt the rhythms of others. Music also helps our brains to release chemicals that produce trust and foster emotional bonding, arousing shared feelings of identity. Because music is deeply related to our place of birth, our childhood experiences, and our family traditions, it is also deeply rooted in our sense of self and belonging. This can be a beautiful experience, but it also means that music can be used for sectarian purposes.[3]

According to Higgins, certain types of music might be used as a badge of identity—think of the way opera, for example, is associated with a certain socioeconomic class, while British punk is associated with a different one. Those who would hope to manipulate the masses understand this and use music to "undercut or sow hostility toward groups." Because human brains love binaries, when we feel these deep feelings of belonging, we seem to almost automatically fall into an "us or them" framework. "Music associated with 'home' can stir feelings of patriotic love of one's 'people,'" while fostering antagonistic thoughts about others.[4] Meanwhile, music that is understood as foreign or alien can reinforce a person's self-identification with their own group, further fostering sectarian belief systems. And because music is not just heard but felt inside our bodies as vibration, it can spur us on to action, to actively moving our bodies—whether that's bopping our head in the car, dancing (or protesting) in the streets, or, in a scarier example, murdering someone we consider not part of our in-group.

CHRISTIAN NATIONALISM, PATRIOTIC HYMNS, AND A GLOBAL CITIZENRY

If music can so powerfully affect our emotions and sense of identity, it makes sense that governments or oppressive bodies might want to use music to manipulate the masses toward patriotism. Unfortunately, nationalism and militarism have crept into many Christian hymns ("Onward, Christian Soldiers," anyone?), fostering not just an alignment with the Christian identity, but a militant one at that. Hymns that speak of militaristic subjects like warfare, victory, soldiers, battle, and fortresses must also, by default, speak of an enemy, a loser, a captive, an evildoer. While it may feel pretty amazing to be on the side of a conquering army marching victorious (something the biblical writers also enjoyed, imagining God's ultimate victory over those who rule over God's people on earth), that also means that there is a people who are conquered, rather than a world in which war and conquest itself are defeated. Music, in this way, becomes an extension of the claim that history is written by the victor. The problem is that Jesus did not generally identify with the conquerors.

"Onward, Christian Soldiers" makes it clear whose side Jesus is on—after all, he's the one carrying the flag into battle. Martin Luther's classic hymn "A Mighty Fortress Is Our God" makes the same claim with the words "Were not the right man on our side / the man of God's own choosing. . . . / and he must win the battle." Contemporary Christian music is no less warlike; Christy Nockels released a song, "A Mighty Fortress," which makes it clear that not only is Jesus on our side but that we'll reign with him upon our victory: The lyrics speak of God as not just a fortress and a refuge but as a kingdom with which we will reign—in other words, we'll share power with God.[5]

Similarly, nationalistic hymns that seem to align our country with God's abundance and blessing are problematic for a few reasons. First, they seem to acknowledge only prosperity without acknowledging communal sin, as if God might turn a blind eye to our national transgressions and fill our coffers anyway. Second, they ignore the victims of our wrongdoings; they do not acknowledge the enslaved, the marginalized, the hurting. Third, they assume a special place in God's heart for our country over others, which increases the potential for xenophobia and anti-immigration sentiment—which is decidedly antithetical to the gospel. "God of Our Fathers, Whose Almighty Hand" speaks of God's protection from war and pestilence as well as a "bounteous goodness" that "nourish[es] us in peace."[6] Hymns such as this one ignore the fact that not everyone was living a life in which goodness was bountiful or peace nourished (not to mention, God might be for mothers, too). At the time this hymn was written, slavery had been abolished for only eleven years and the formerly enslaved had received no reparations (although the slave owners did) and lived in poverty. Meanwhile, the United States government, in its lust for gold, was violently reneging on the treaties it had signed with Indigenous tribes in the West. Bounteous goodness was only for the White man, which many nationalistic hymns conveniently ignore.

On July 4, 2017, Dallas's First Baptist Church Choir sang a new song by Gary Moore, "Make America Great Again," in front of a huge American flag.[7] Though the simple lyrics don't mention God specifically, seeing the all-White choir sing it in church communicates a clear message: God is going to make America great again, because we're God's favorite. It's also true that the slogan "Make America Great Again" is a racist dog whistle that harks back to the days of segregation and Jim Crow. Of course, nationalism is not unbiblical; the Bible is filled with warring nations and a fight to preserve a national identity. (This is why I often chuckle when people claim they don't want their Christianity to be political.)

The question for those who follow Jesus, however, is where his alignment would have been—and I don't think it's with a Caesar of any sort. The biblical narrative, after all, is the story of a conquered people—it is that people's resistance literature. It's natural, I think, for a conquered people to fantasize about victory. The psalmists certainly did! Even the disciples fell victim to this mistake about what Jesus was here to do. But when we fall too deeply into that daydream, we start to miss the point.

Of course, if we claim kinship with Jesus and alliance with the realm of God, rather than the plane of earthly principalities, we are claiming a sort of "cosmic identity," but it's possible to do that in a way that, as those Methodist clergy insisted at their conference, offers everyone a place at the table. Rather than singing songs that sound like national anthems—which are more often than not expressions of violence and dominance—we can also begin to understand the types of hymns that might better represent the beloved community and the realm of God of which we want to be a part. A song that demonstrates a Christian's allegiance—a citizenship in the realm of God and not some sort of patriarchal, colonizing "kingdom"—will be more concerned with the spiritual and physical well-being of all people, as well as justice that is real and true. These songs will lift up mercy over vengeance or victory, and most importantly will abhor war and our alignment with violence and dominance as a sense of identity.

A hymn or anthem aligned with the realm of God is one that values a global citizenry. It boasts a reliance on God, but not as though God were taking sides. Rather, it portrays a humility that demonstrates that if we are on God's side, serving God's will, the world we create will be more about peace and justice than war and violence. If we examine the overarching narrative of the Bible as a whole, and the Jesus story as part of that narrative that we deeply value, we cannot honestly claim citizenship in God's realm if we are not willing to hold in our own embodiment a bent toward justice, a cry for mercy, and a dogged determination to obtain equity for the oppressed. This means the best songs of praise, worship, or lament will show concern for all of God's creation—not just the parts that look like us. In order to do this well, we must seek out not songs that align with the powerful, the rich, the mighty, but rather music that includes the meek, invites the lonely, and resists the colonizing oppressor.

WHAT THAT SONG REALLY MEANT

(Bryana)

In September 1814, during the War of 1812, Francis Scott Key, a thirty-five-year-old lawyer, sailed on a ship flying a truce flag to negotiate with the British Royal Navy to free his friend, a popular doctor. While on the ship, Key witnessed the bombardment of Fort McHenry. At dawn the next day, he learned that America had won the battle. He saw the American flag waving over the fort, and that inspired him to write a poem that was later set to an existing tune and ended up becoming "The Star-Spangled Banner."

Kerry mentioned earlier how easy it is for her to sing along to a song without paying close attention to the lyrics. I can recall many times I have done the same thing ("Walk This Way" by Aerosmith?! That's news to me!). While I'm not an Aerosmith fan—it's just not my favorite genre of music—if I ever hear that song again, I will always be conscious of its true meaning, and if I have a choice, I will turn it off. But what about songs that have more complicated lyrics, or are less obviously problematic? "The Star-Spangled Banner" is one of those less obvious songs. As a child and young adult, I remember singing it at every football game, with my right hand on my chest, gazing at the American flag. We are socialized to believe this is one of the most patriotic songs in America. So let's unpack the history for a minute.

During the War of 1812, the British promised refuge to any enslaved people who escaped their enslavers, which, as you can imagine, really pissed off White Americans. They feared losing their free labor over-night and also feared large-scale revolts by African Americans who were enslaved. The British kept their promise after the war, and refused to return the African and African American marines to America.

The second half of Key's third verse ends like this:

> No refuge could save the hireling and slave
> From the terror of flight or the gloom of the grave,
> And the star-spangled banner in triumph doth wave
> O'er the land of the free and the home of the brave.

I often talk about how important historical context is to understanding the manifestation of White power and privilege in today's institutions. It is no different with music. With this history in mind, reread the lyrics above. What do you think Key meant by "no refuge could save the hireling and slave / From the terror of flight or the gloom of the grave"? What might you think, now, of Black athletes like Colin Kaepernick kneeling at football games during the singing of the national anthem?

These lyrics are clearly meant to scorn and threaten the African Americans who took the British up on their offer, Jefferson Morley, author of *Snow-Storm in August: Washington City, Francis Scott Key, and the Forgotten Race Riot of 1835,* wrote in an essay for the *Washington Post.*[8] Francis Scott Key was descended from a wealthy plantation family and he himself enslaved people. Through his public career, Key opposed emancipation unless the freed people of color were imme-diately sent to Africa. "The Negroes," Key wrote, are "a distinct and inferior race of people, which all experience prove to be the greatest evil that afflicts a community."[9] From 1833 to 1840, Key served as the chief law enforcement officer in the nation's capital and presided over the daily enforcement of enslavement laws.

In his essay, Morley reminds us that it wasn't until after the Civil War that "The Star-Spangled Banner" was adopted by Southerners as a symbol of the end of the Reconstruction era, when the federal government defended the constitutional rights of African Americans. Whenever controversy arose over the song (for reasons other than its White supremacist lyrics), the Veterans of Foreign Wars and the United Daughters of the Confederacy responded in fierce opposition. If your first instinct is to defend a song because it doesn't have overtly racist undertones, it's important to consider the author of the lyrics, the social dynamics of the era in which the song was written, and from what perspective it was written (perspective of the dominant culture or the marginalized culture). Music has a powerful impact on our emotions and sense of identity. As a leader in your church community, it is important to consider the ways your music may divide and oppress as well as the ways in which it can uplift and empower.

We answer to a higher authority than civic tradition. Some of you may recall the many times when the public discourse was driven by opposition to "alternative" patriotic anthems. One such alternative is "Lift Every Voice and Sing," often referred to as the Black National Anthem and frequently sung in Black churches and schools and even in a few landmark performances, like Beyoncé at Coachella.

LIFTING UP VOICES OF RESISTANCE

(Bryana and Kerry)

"Lift Ev'ry Voice and Sing" was composed by two brothers from Jacksonville, Florida. James Weldon Johnson composed the poem in 1899 and John Rosamond Johnson set it to music in 1900.[10] It was written during the time of Jim Crow, and eventually became the official song of the NAACP. Let's unpack this song, using the three key points in early Jewish resistance poetry set forth by Mark Medley of Baptist Seminary of Kentucky.[11] First, a poem of resistance sings a counter-discourse to empire and imperial oppression, while praising God and reinforcing a communal identity, as in the first verse:[12]

> Lift ev'ry voice and sing
> Till earth and Heaven ring,
> Ring with the harmonies of liberty.
> Let our rejoicing rise
> High as the listening skies;
> Let it resound as loud as the rolling sea.
> Sing a song full of the faith that the dark Past has taught us,
> Sing a song full of the hope that the present has brought us.
> Facing the rising sun of our new day begun,
> Let us march on, till victory is won.

According to Shana L. Redmond, author of two books and a professor of musicology and African American studies at UCLA, "the 'Liberty' of which James Weldon Johnson wrote included the rights and protections that citizens of African descent in the United States were promised but had yet to receive."[13]

Second, the song remembers past events as a reminder to never forget the suffering and obstacles of the past.

> Stony the road we trod,
> Bitter the chastening rod,
> Felt in the days when hope unborn had died.
> Yet, with a steady beat,
> Have not our weary feet
> Come to the place for which our fathers sighed?
> We have come over a way that with tears has been watered;
> We have come, treading our path through the blood of the
>   slaughtered,
> Out from the gloomy past,
> Till now we stand at last
> Where the white gleam of our bright star is cast.

The "chastening rod" refers to the brutal whippings endured by Africans and African Americans who were enslaved on plantations. The blood alludes to lynching and other violence endured by Black people throughout the nineteenth and twentieth centuries.

Third, the song articulates an imagined hope for the future.[14]

> God of our weary years,
> God of our silent tears,
> Thou who has brought us thus far on the way;
> Thou who hast by thy might
> Led us into the light,
> Keep us forever in the path, we pray.

Singing can be both a subversive act of resistance and a clarion call for a new way to be in the world. When you think about the powerful ways in which music can forge identities, bolster group bonding, and inspire people into action, the importance of the way we talk about God and the oppressed in our music becomes paramount. Medley notes, "Songs and singing can . . . be powerful political instruments. They give expression to dissent, protesting the structures, systems and values of a dominant society, and they shape the collective identity of people participating in social and political movements."[15] In other words, when your church begins to sing the songs of the resistance, not only will you be announcing to the world that you stand for the oppressed and the marginalized, but your congregants will also begin to identify as people who are part of the justice movement.

For our churches to sing lyrics such as those found in Mark Miller's "Child of God,"[16] which tell us that nothing can change the fact that we are all divine offspring, is far more representative of the beloved community than images of victors and fortresses, especially considering that modern-day militant rhetoric is very much concerned with who should be kept out—out of our country's borders, out of gendered bathrooms, out of pulpits. Rather than identifying with militant victors marching through the streets in a display of might and power, people who absorb songs of the resistance will align themselves with those who have been oppressed and invite them into a beautiful new collective. In White Christian America, this is an important paradigm shift.

I know it may feel uncomfortable to think that your church music should be so political, but again, I assert that the Bible is a deeply political document, and resistance runs through its syllables from the first letter of Genesis through the last line of Revelation. The Jewish psalter is often a mixture of praise and protest, crying out to God both in worship and for justice. The resistance poetry of Second Temple Judaism both resists empire and promotes Jewish identity. According to Medley, early Jewish resistance poetry follows three key points. First, it remembers past events; second, it sings a counter-discourse to empire and imperial oppression while praising God and reinforcing a communal identity; and third, it articulates an imagined hope for the future. We can use these three points as guides in our own musical selections.[17]

The tricky thing about empire is its ubiquitous nature. When something is everywhere, it's hard to resist, because its subliminal messaging eases its way into our brain cells with virtually no effort—or even awareness—on our part. This is exactly how empire wants it. This is also what makes songs of protest so powerful—they shine a spotlight on that which would prefer to remain hidden in plain sight. The Jews and the early Christians living in first-century Palestine experienced this phenomenon, too. The Roman Empire was everywhere in the pop culture of the day, be it the art that lined the streets or the songs sung, well, everywhere. Hymns were a form of indoctrination.[18] That's what makes the hymns written by the early Christians so subversive—they co-opted the tool of the oppressor and used it against imperial forces to assert their own identity in a world of social hybridity.

SO NOW WHAT DO WE DO?

Some of you may be panicking right now, thinking about all the ways in which you have inadvertently aligned yourselves with empire and dominance by singing the beloved hymns and praise music of your childhood. Others of you may be thinking, "Hey, we're better off than I thought." In either case, there are some nuances to keep in mind when it comes to being musically anti-racist.

From everything we've discussed so far, you probably already recognize that a solid audit of your cache of go-to hymns needs to be performed with a merciless eye looking for anything that aligns with empire and dominance. For any music that's performed, it's a good idea to have more than one person's eyes on it, and if possible, at least some of those eyes should belong to BIPOC. There needs to be a regular procedure in which music is reviewed for its theology and ideology so you and your team can identify what messages are being sent through your music. In addition to the blatantly warlike hymns you'll want to avoid, you also want to be on the lookout for more subtle messaging that reinforces supremacy, such as lyrics that perpetuate the "darkness is evil" paradigm. You'll also be searching for those hymns that are more justice oriented—and they are out there. There are indeed songs being written that can help your congregation "sing their way toward justice and toward the truth about oppression, prejudice, and respect for diversity."[19] But there's more to think about than just the lyrics. We have to be very careful about the way we go about the performance of these songs, too.

Many White churches might rush to sing gospel music as a way to appear cool, hip, and welcoming to Black folk, but this type of **performative justice** is no real justice at all. If your church is not doing the real work of manifesting justice for Black people but is singing music that arose out of Black culture and struggle, your work is empty and will fall flat. I can't imagine anything much more insulting than a bunch of middle-class White people singing "We Shall Overcome" while not simultaneously working to divest themselves of the privilege that protects them from the oppression that Black people are working to resist. If you are singing songs in Spanish about liberation but not doing work in the world to make your community safer for the Latinx community (and yes, that means humane treatment for refugees and sincere welcome for immigrants, thank you very much), your music program is one of those clanging gongs that apparently bugged the heck out of the apostle Paul.[20] The point is, you don't get to *sing* justice if you're not willing to *do* justice and to existentially *be* justice oriented.

Who gets to perform is important, too. Divesting yourself of privilege and power means surrendering space for Black and Brown bodies to take leadership over aspects of our worship, and we rejoice when they do it in ways that are different from how we would do it (even if that makes us and/or our congregation uncomfortable). Redistributing funds to pay BIPOC musicians is a wonderful way to intentionally support Black and Brown musicians economically, expose your church to music that is more representative, and do it in an authentic way.

PERFORMANCE WITHOUT JUSTICE
(Josh)

Matt is a close friend and is easily one of the best musicians in the city. He sings and plays the piano with an anointing I have not seen on many others. Matt is a child of the Black church and, most importantly, loves to worship with the people of God. I can't help but think of Matt when processing, as Kerry said, churches who *sing* justice but do not *do* justice.

Matt had a curiosity for the vision I shared of an integrated church pursuing racial justice and was willing to step away from services that offered him financial compensation to guide my predominantly White church free of charge. The church I was working for had many skilled musicians, who agreed that diversifying music style and content would be a catalyst for moving the church toward embodying racial justice. So it seemed like a perfect opportunity to invite Matt into this work with us.

The worship leaders' world was starkly White. Their Spotify playlists, car radio stations, and church experience reinforced one way of worship. Whether they were well versed in contemporary Christian music or hymns, the music they knew could only uphold notions of empire and an image of God that is all too commonly found in White pseudosupremacist theology. They needed a guide, and I was convinced Matt could be the one to break into their world and show them a new way of worship.

The first few Sundays with Matt at the helm were almost transcendent. The congregation moved in ways they never had before; they were being invited into a new beautiful stream of worship where we lamented, praised, and sought after a God who could liberate us all. For the first time on staff, I felt a sense of belonging that had been elusive for me since entering this faith community. But soon enough the dream began to crumble. The congregation loved having Matt lead worship, and they loved this new music style and how it moved their bodies. While their love for the music was immense, their love for Matt was not as much. Far too often, congregants would approach Matt, who had become a regular attendee of the church, to ask if he was playing that week. The conversation nearly always stopped there if he replied with a no. Very few were interested in who Matt was or why he even considered attending this church. He no longer was a guide but a bridge to their new and exciting worship experience. Matt's very body became a tool for them to experience something foreign and different. He was never engaged as a member of this congregation; his voice and his hands were all that mattered. His tremendous generosity to turn down paid opportunities at his home church in order to play for free at my church was taken advantage of and turned into a minstrel show under the guise of racial reconciliation.

The church never gave Matt a chance to bring his full self into the community, and as time progressed, even what he was allowed to bring in was contained. Some had complained we had strayed too far from the "normal" worship style and needed to adjust. The result was a limit on the number of gospel songs played per month and a rejection of music that could be performed in other languages or cultural expressions. Matt was limited in the songs he was allowed to lead worship with, while White worship leaders had no such limitations. He had to stretch more than any other worship leader, playing music outside of his norm while the rest of the worship leaders were not asked to step outside of theirs.

Matt and I would regularly meet over a meal to unpack and for me to listen to what was happening behind the scenes. Deep grief, anger, and shame washed over me during these meals. I love Matt and wanted this brother to be safe and welcomed into this community of faith. But we could not bring this church to look beyond the entertainment value of Matt's music and talent to see the deeper opportunities for their holy discomfort. Worship was for the White congregants, and everyone else had to adjust themselves to fit their expression of it. Instead of seeing worship as an opportunity for more profound solidarity with the BIPOC family in God, it was for their White edification and enjoyment.

Worship is such a powerful space for belonging, expressing hospitality to communities different from our own, and making space for others to experience these same sentiments.[21] This process of making space cannot happen when Whiteness determines who belongs and the amount of space BIPOC can take up. When Whiteness is driving the worship experience, we run into the threat of **cultural appropriation.** Instead of being authentically performed, BIPOC music and art is claimed by the White congregation as their own, which either distorts the original expression or erases the presence of BIPOC from the experience.

The fleeting moments that centered our Blackness came during worship times, but as those moments became less and less, the urge to leave to find spaces for belonging—instead of only being seen as entertainment—grew. Matt and I would ultimately end up leaving that church around the same time. He was never fully compensated for the training he offered to worship leaders, worship consulting, and coaching church leaders on multicultural worship. He never did feel as if he belonged. The burden of being Black in a White church took a heavy toll on his spirit, which led to his departure.

I wish stories like these were outliers, but unfortunately, they are all too common. Multicultural worship is difficult but immensely beautiful. If we are willing to decenter Whiteness in the process and use worship as a tool to cultivate solidarity with our BIPOC neighbors, we can start to manifest justice in our churches.

ASSESSMENT 3.1: MUSIC SELECTION AND PERFORMANCE

1. Where do you experience resistance to expressing different cultural styles of worship? What are the barriers within your church to differences in worship?
2. What is the source of your music? Is it exclusively CCLI or certain hymnbooks?
3. Who performs the majority of your music? Can they authentically perform your musical choices?
4. Who is the final authority on what music is performed and by whom? Do they use an anti-racist lens when making their decisions?

5. How can you recognize when your music is being authentically performed compared to being performed as **cultural appropriation**? Do you know?

ASSESSMENT 3.2: MUSICAL THEMES AND MESSAGING

1. What types of images do your musical selections portray? Are any of the following militaristic or nationalistic images included? Are there others not included on this list?

   — Nations/Allegiances
   — Victory
   — Soldiers
   — Battle
   — Fortresses
   — Nationalistic blessing / abundance
   — Banners and flags
   — Defense/protection

2. Do themes of abundance and prosperity in your music include everyone or do they ignore the suffering of some marginalized groups (for example, immigrants, BIPOC who live in fear of the police, Palestinians living under Israeli rule, Jewish Americans attending synagogue in fear of gun violence)?
3. What songs (if any) do you currently include that demonstrate themes of inclusion for all and solidarity with the marginalized?
4. Do any of your songs promote a global ethos of inclusivity, or do they perpetuate nationalist borders?

4
Small Groups

If church is about community, then nowhere does the nuts and bolts of what it means to be in relationship happen more intensely than at your weekly small group. If my elementary school days taught me anything, it's that groupthink and social dynamics are compelling factors in our sense of belonging and self-esteem, and there's nothing like a second grader's birthday party to let you know whether you're part of the in or the out group. (Trust me. I have the therapy bills to prove it.)

Just because we're grown-ups now doesn't necessarily mean we play well with others any better than we did back in the day. It's not that we don't want to be awesome grown-ups. It's just that we're probably better at holding fast to the stereotypes, social mores, and status quo that make us feel supercomfortable than we are at dismantling them. After all, they've become nice and familiar, like a cozy blanket we can wrap ourselves in whenever we're feeling insecure. What makes these deep beliefs and motivations insidious, however, is that within them lie all the racist tropes we rightfully love to hate, but they're buried deep and usually only come out in those frustrating awkward social moments where someone in the room is left thinking, "Wait, did he mean what I *think* he meant by that comment?" For people who are not a member of the dominant identity, these awkward moments are not just cringeworthy; they are utterly exhausting and possibly dangerous.

Who knew your small group could be such a sociological minefield?

There's more to think about here, too. When it comes to our sense of belonging and identity, self-esteem and agency, the small groups we move through play a big part of who we are and how we show up in the world. When it comes to small groups officiated and institutionalized by the church, it's important to understand that they are an extension of the pulpit, the long arm of the church that reaches into the intimate living space of the congregant. As such, small groups hold the power of both the legitimacy of the establishment and the influence of intimacy and vulnerability. I'm thinking of Josh's friend Matt, who was only ever seen for what he could offer the congregation musically. Being seen in a relationship can feel scary and vulnerable, and it can also be empowering and transformative. But in order for it to not do harm—especially as an extension of the church—it's important that small-group leaders understand a little about group dynamics, power structures, and the way empire can sneak in through even the most well-monitored cracks.

RACIALIZED CONTEXTS IN ALL-WHITE SPACES

Before we dive into the psychology of groupthink, there's a point I need to make about **racialized contexts**: racialized events can occur even in spaces where there are no BIPOC to be found. Because White people often don't think of ourselves as having a racial identity (we're just "normal," whatever *that* means) we never think about the way Whiteness is at play in any given situation. Subtle—and sometimes, not so subtle—acts of racism can occur in all-White spaces, and too often, White people remain silent. Of course, a racist thing isn't racist only when there are BIPOC in the vicinity, but if there are no BIPOC in the room, there's less pressure to perform justice. A *true* sense of justice and anti-racism that is existential—who you are, not just what you perform—will be practiced even in the Whitest spaces you roll through.

What does a racialized context look like in an all-White small group? A racialized context or event *is any space or event at which racial dynamics cause either inner or outer conflict, whether implicitly or explicitly.* Microaggressions are excellent examples of the sort of racialized event that might occur in a small group where there are mixed racial identities, but the conflict can result even in spaces that are all White, and in which the White people are staying silent. For example, when one White person tells a racist joke or promotes a racist stereotype, other

A SPECIAL NOTE ON ANTI-RACISM TASK FORCES (BRYANA)

It has become very popular, within many church contexts, to form small groups centered around "dismantling racism." Sometimes they are called "task forces." Other times they are called "committees." It typically starts with yet another lynching of *another* innocent Black person at the hands of police. We see Black Lives Matter protesters on the news, and depending on the news station we are watching, we may even hear them referred to as rioters (an example of the perpetuation of racism via our media channels, but that's a story for another day). It's like clockwork. White leaders have no idea what to do, but they know they have to do *something,* so they appoint a few people from their congregation who have a passion for racial justice (never mind whether they are equipped to do justice work or not), and if they are lucky, they are able to recruit one "token" BIPOC to be a part of this task force. Most of the time these committees are relegated to the basement of the church (literally, or at least metaphorically) and are not given any direction other than the title of their committee: "dismantle racism."

In my experience, these groups get to work right away. They facilitate book studies and they plan gatherings to watch and discuss videos on the topics of race and racism. They do a lot of performative allyship. They spend a lot of time creating spaces for the majority (White people) to reflect on their Whiteness. These spaces, in many cases, become therapy sessions for White guilt and maybe even White shock over the atrocities of America's racist past and present. Unfortunately, this is as far as a lot of these committees go. Despite good intentions, they end up tokenizing Black people, perpetuating racism through White tears, and creating harmful spaces for BIPOC. At the end of the day, authentic commitment to racial equity is not accomplished, and more harm than good is inflicted.

Let's examine what authentic anti-racism looks like in the construction of task forces like these. Following are some important considerations if you plan to create an anti-racism task force, as well as some guiding questions.

Create meaningful goals and objectives of the task force. Ask yourselves important questions, such as:

— Why do we want to create a task force in the first place?
— What do we hope to accomplish by doing so?
— How will we know if we are successful?
— How will we know if we are causing harm?

Strategically appoint the right people to lead and participate in the task force. It is not enough to casually ask a few people who seem to have a passion for racial justice to lead the task force. It is important to ask yourself questions, such as:

— Are the participants and leaders equipped to do the work of racial justice in our church?
— If the answer is no, How can we invest in our people so that they are more equipped to lead?

Sometimes the solution is to invest in race equity consultants to help with this. I promise this is not a sales pitch for my and my fellow authors' businesses! In my experience, it is always worth the investment to get outside help. It is nearly impossible to change a culture from within, without outside perspective and guidance from those who are equipped in race equity culture and care.

There's one more important element to consider, particularly for churches with predominantly White people in their congregation. While BIPOC perspectives are critical to this work, do not put the burden of "dismantling racism" on your BIPOC members! It is not *their* labor. It is the responsibility of White people to do this work. And, more often than not, the work that has to be done first is White awareness of racial identity and systemic racism, and the divestment of White power.

That leads us to a third consideration:

*In order for a Dismantling Racism task force to go beyond **doing** anti-racism work and to **be** anti-racist, it must not be relegated to a "basement committee."* You know, the committees that start with good intentions, or a great idea, and ultimately end up becoming exclusive, or in some cases, fizzling out over time. I speak from experience. I was the "token" Black person leading a Dismantling Racism task force for a predominantly White congregation. The church leaders at the time publicly communicated their commitment to racial equity work and used the task force as proof of that commitment. It took us months to get equity initiatives approved, and many initiatives never got the green light. The committee was often met with hostility and defensiveness by church staff and leadership. While the committee looked good on paper, members spent hours strategizing, advocating, and facilitating meetings, often without any significant progress. The committee was never given actual power to influence and make decisions. It was consistently blocked from doing what it was intended to do. In fact, it caused more harm for the few BIPOC involved, and ultimately made little progress. It was a "basement committee."

— *How will you invest in your committee?*
— *What resources (time, space, financial, human) will be accessible to your committee to ensure its success?*
— *From what other projects might you be willing to divest resources in order to properly equip the anti-racism committee?*

*Determine if the Dismantling Racism task force is authentic rather than performative by interrogating whether the outward expression of the work is reflective of the **actual work being done within.*** Chances are, if you have a predominantly White church, with mostly or all White leadership and staff, your goal probably shouldn't include becoming a multiracial congregation, for example. There are a few reasons for this. In various places throughout this book, we mention that sometimes, BIPOC need BIPOC-only spaces. There are African American churches for a reason. BIPOC need safe spaces where they can be their authentic selves without threat of being minimized, without having to respond to White tears, and where they get to choose what best serves their needs, including how they want to worship. Also, if you don't have any BIPOC leaders or staff, or if you've had BIPOC leaders or staff in the past, but they didn't stay, there's a reason for that. One of your first goals should be to interrogate that reality:

— *Why haven't we questioned this before?*
— *Why are our leaders and staff predominantly White?*
— *What is the history of this church in its active role (silence and complicity counts as an active role) in White pseudosupremacy and racism?*

If you have BIPOC leaders or members of the Dismantling Racism team, the best thing you can do to ensure it thrives is to get out of the way. **Do not interrupt disruption.** In other words, White people, divest yourselves of power. Redistribute funds. Submit to BIPOC leadership and trust BIPOC self-agency and ability to guide race equity vision, mission, goals, and actions. Remove bureaucracy in decision making. Let go of the need for the White pseudosupremacist lie of perfection. Give up the need to control, and finally, give up the (conscious or subconscious) idea that "White is right" and trust the power and leadership of BIPOC. If you can do those things, your Dismantling Racism committee may stand a chance of making transformative change.

ASSESSMENT 4.1: AUTHENTIC RACE-EQUITY INITIATIVES

1. Is your church hosting book clubs and video discussions, but everyone continues to be stuck when it comes to actual action? If yes, consider focusing on White racial identity development first. How can you provide spaces for White people to unpack their own identity as racial beings, focusing on inward action first, before outward action?
2. Are you announcing on your website and social media accounts that you are committed to the work, but you have invested very little money in supporting local (or national) Black organizations and Black leaders doing the work? If yes, identify ways you need to financially support your racial equity commitments. It is easy to tell what is important to any organization by looking at where their money goes.
3. Do you have a very small percentage—if any—of financial investment budgeted for inner work, such as assessments and regular training for leaders and staff, and even congregational members? If yes, consider an investment in training for staff, leadership, and congregational members as one (very important) example of a financial commitment in racial equity.
4. Do you have language in your Dismantling Racism covenant (if you have one) that articulates a goal of becoming a multiracial (or cultural) congregation?

White people in the room who fiercely disagree with not only the joke but also the telling of it might remain silent in order to maintain a semblance of comfort and avoid confrontation. The ones staying silent are not actually comfortable themselves. In fact, they (we) tend to be deeply uncomfortable with blatant displays of racist ignorance. Yet the power of the group causes us to adhere to unspoken rules of racialized "etiquette" that keep us from confronting the behavior. We'll get to why that happens in a minute.

The racism we experience in all-White spaces can be ridiculously blatant or incredibly subtle, but we all know when it's happening. What's important is what happens next—will the other White people in the room choose to be anti-racist and confront what happened, or will we all stay silent? A racialized context or event becomes a **racist context or event** *when the racist act is not confronted, called out, and dismantled by White people.* When racialized events occur in mixed groups and it's left to the BIPOC in the room to confront it, it's still a racist event because the White people are leaving the labor of anti-racism to BIPOC. Either way, whether in mixed or all-White spaces, if White people are not confronting racist comments or actions, White silence is in action. White silence is complicity, and complicity is racist.

WHY SO QUIET? THE POWER DYNAMICS BEHIND WHITE SILENCE

There's a difference between position and influence. Good leaders often have both. Not-so-great leaders usually just have the title. Great leaders, though, are people who can lack the authority of a coveted position and still have influence over their organization. On the flip side, if you've ever worked in an office you've probably experienced the negative side of social influence—that one office troublemaker who loves to stir the pot with gossip or general negativity. These folks can make life miserable for everyone, and they don't even need to have a position of authority to do it—all they need is enough influence over a few people to wreak their havoc.

So, what's at play here? It's a power dynamic.

The first thing to consider about small-group dynamics is the difference between power *over* and power *to*. To be an institution that truly embodies anti-racism, it's important that we divest ourselves of *power over* and work to equitably distribute the *power to*. For diverse churches, this means making sure that our BIPOC members have access to meaningful leadership positions that can enact influence over corporate governance. For White churches working to be anti-racist, empowering anti-racist voices means creating spaces that cultivate the safety of White people who challenge the status quo and confront racism when it happens.

The first step in doing this is to have a clearly worded anti-racist policy that is publicly available to everyone. Not only does this help your church self-identify as anti-racist, but it also helps inform the social mores of your organization. It helps people understand what sorts of language, behavior, and attitudes are acceptable. The second step is to have an escalation process in place that helps people understand not just what's acceptable, but what to do when something falls out of bounds. Though this will always be contextual to an extent, you'll want to have a general idea of how you will respond to a racial crisis should one occur within your organization. This will help everyone—BIPOC and White people—feel safer in confronting racist behavior should it happen within your organization.

Before I go any further, let me say that I know and acknowledge that the safety of White people who call out racism is not really an issue here. Let's face it—telling dear Aunt Sally over coffee and cake in your living room that her racist tropes and stereotypes are not funny and are actually quite harmful is hardly the same as taking a rubber bullet in a street protest (although I'm not beyond asking us to do that as well). By "safety" here, we're talking about the *perceived* threat of social isolation from our peer or family group—that's a very real thing, and our brains are literally telling us we might die if we insult Aunt Sally. And this is the crux of the matter when it comes to small-group dynamics: we fear exclusion from the group if we challenge the status quo. This fear response is the thing in us that we need to practice agency over.

Research shows that within social relationships, human beings will categorize ourselves and each other and then coordinate our behavior according to these categories. The two primary categories in which we place people instantaneously are race and gender, and then we operate based on alleged "common knowledge" (cultural codes of social difference, also known as racist and sexist stereotypes) to determine their place in the social hierarchies that we all fall into. What's tricky about all of this is that these standards of "common knowledge" (i.e., stereotypes) are based on culturally essentialized traits.[1] In other words, we imagine that all people of a certain race or gender have these traits inherently (think about the ridiculous stereotypes of Black athleti-cism, White intelligence, and female nurturing). The thing about these essentialized traits, however, is that they are formed and shaped by the dominant culture. In other words, straight White men decided what the rest of us essentially are and pigeonholed us all to live up to or resist those standards.

Here's the real kicker, though, and it's a big one that helps explain groupthink: because these beliefs play such a big role in how we cat-egorize ourselves and each other, they also determine how we behave in social settings like a church's small groups, and thus play a big part in how we organize ourselves and behave in social settings.[2] But the power here doesn't lie in the fact that individuals believe them, but rather in a person's belief that *most* people believe them, and that there are some sort of public rules by which they will be judged and expected to act. That's why when one racist jerk spouts nonsense in a room, and every-one else in the room recognizes that this person is a jerk, they all stay silent because they think everyone *else* agrees with the jerk.

But what makes the jerk so powerful that everyone will let them keep going? The answer is something sociologists call **cost reduction**, defined as "*a process involving changes in values (personal, social, eco-nomic) which reduces the pains incurred in meeting the demands of a pow-erful other.*"[3] Because our need to belong to a group (a biological drive for safety held over from our infancy) is so strong, we are conditioned to weigh the cost of speaking up. Do I risk being cast out of the safety of the group for my anti-racist values? Is that a cost I'm willing to pay?

Let's consider an example that so many White people experience: a family gathering with a relative known for making racist jokes. White people are intensely aware that, considering complex family dynam-ics, there is a risk that they will be ostracized if they resist the racism happening at the dinner table. There is a risk that not only will din-ner become intensely uncomfortable, but their family of origin may become angry with them. Relationships might actually be damaged—in some cases, irreparably. We will weigh this risk and often decide that we are not willing to pay that cost. This is cost reduction in action, and it's a real phenomenon with real consequences.

For BIPOC the risk and the cost are far more dire. White people are often upset by racist Uncle Joe's stupid jokes, but they are not an assault on our actual being. At worst they are assaults on people we love: life partners, children, friends. But our own embodiment and emotional well-being remains relatively safe. Even if you are married to or parent a BIPOC, if you are White, the risk and the cost are far less than our Black and Brown siblings must consider in the same types of situations. When they experience a racist event, the risk they weigh often includes their embodied safety—and sometimes, their very lives. All of these decisions are based on coddling the emotions of the dominant identities in the room in order to keep the peace. And keeping the peace is exactly what cost reduction is designed to do.

For many of the churches I work with, cost reduction is where resistance begins. There will inevitably be some sort of sentiment like, "We have to speak about this in a way that people will listen, otherwise they will just leave." While I agree that screaming (even if only metaphorically) is pointless and no way to convince anyone of anything, my answer to these comments is always the same: Even if you're as nice as you can be in your anti-racism work, *there will be a cost.* If you're hoping to engage in this work without having some really uncomfortable conversations—and possibly even losing relationships with a few beloved members—you are probably doing it wrong. As any good change management consultant will tell you, you can probably expect 20 percent of your congregation to leave. At the same time, by becoming holistically anti-racist (which is what this book is designed to help you do) you will not just help companion many of your members on the journey of their racial deconstruction, but you'll also most likely attract many others who care deeply about this work. Best of all, when that happens, you'll become a church that will actually be safe for BIPOC, and maybe your dreams of diversity will come true in a way that is healthy and just, not just performative.

Cost reduction will generally "deepen and stabilize social relations over and above the condition of balance."[4] In other words, it maintains the status quo and keeps a false sense of peace, and the collateral damage is equity and justice. White people have reduced the cost to ourselves by maintaining a false sense of peace and staying silent, even if most of us in the room think that one racist dude is a jerk.

To balance social relations, therefore, requires destabilization of the current hierarchy. We need to examine the culture we are cultivating, especially in our small groups, because these are the places our power dynamics play out in the realm of the interpersonal. This is great practice for us to identify where we practice agency over our own biases, where we speak truth to power, and where we find the inner courage to confront dangerous ideologies that do harm. For some of us who have more diverse churches, we can divest ourselves of power and create more welcoming groups by submitting to BIPOC leadership of our small-group curriculum and culture. We can be more intentional about selecting curricula that are less aligned with empire and more aligned with the marginalized. In order to do this, we need to cultivate an eye for the ways in which empire and the qualities of Whiteness (for example, the way our worth and value as humans seems tied to our productivity rather than our humanity) sneak into our Bible studies and small-group curriculum. Whenever possible, we should submit to BIPOC wisdom in order to do this well.

THE LANGUAGE OF PSEUDOSUPREMACY: WHITENESS IN SMALL-GROUP CURRICULUM

(Josh)

Your church, like many North American churches, may structure small-group experiences around a curriculum. In our digital age, there are so many options for curricula! Denominations, Christian publishers, and church planting networks all have their versions, and while I cannot tell you which to choose, I can help you learn to recognize how White pseudosupremacy manifests itself in church content in both seemingly harmless *and* overtly racist ways.

Many discipleship resources transmit a nuanced White pseudosupremacy by reinforcing harmful racialized narratives. Early on in one of the books used by several churches I have collaborated with, the author writes about how language shapes culture, using 1990s hip-hop as an example of how violent language creates violent cultures. The author writes that because of the violent shared language, the entire worldview and culture were violent as well. While 1990s hip-hop was not free of beef and conflict in both lyrics and real life, defining an entire culture and worldview by that violence is inaccurate and is a commonly racist trope. Instead of naming parts of White culture that are inherently violent, like the KKK and segregationist Citizens' Councils, the author conjures the image of violent Black men with his hip-hop reference.

Another example is so egregious I must quote it directly. The White pastor-author speaks on God's purpose for labor and says: "When people become unemployed it's as though they have fallen from their God-given call to lead productive lives. . . . The focus of productivity and fruitfulness in their lives is lost; it's as though they stop being fully human."[5] Cringey, right? If I remember correctly, Jesus quit his job as a carpenter to travel around with a group of scrubs, and the role of local healer and rabbi was not salaried. When we make work and productivity the values in which we place our worth as image-bearers, our capacity to generate and produce capital then defines how valuable we are. This theological stance boldly proclaims that those who don't hold a job in the formal economy (the formerly incarcerated, the differently abled, those experiencing homelessness, sex workers, gig workers) or are unemployed live below their calling and *may not even be fully human.* This "bootstrap mentality" is as well documented as it is flawed. Too many of our neighbors are bootless because of our racialized systems. To then define their humanity by their capacity to produce is harmful and reinforces White pseudosupremacy. This sort of dehumanizing messaging—cloaked in theological language, no less—has no place in the curriculum of a church working to be anti-racist.

Certain vacation Bible school curricula have proven problematic when using other cultures as a "theme." In 2019, one program with an African theme was criticized on social media and even in national publications for some overtly racist content in its activities for kids and how it described other cultures. During one of the program's units, VBS leaders were to pretend to be "mean Egyptian slave drivers" and have kids act as slaves; the leaders were to press them to work harder, and the curriculum even encouraged the leader to call the children "lazy slaves." The program also offered an interactive activity in which the Xhosa language was described as the "clicking language" and encouraged the kids to walk around making clicking noises at one another. Thousands of churches throughout North America purchased this content. The publisher, a major producer of VBS materials, did make some edits and offered a stock apology after some significant pressure but made no mention of the substantive changes needed to keep these problems from reoccurring.

These examples suffer from consistent flaws in White Christian curricula that often go unattended. This flattening and fragmenting of culture is an outgrowth of colonial power and reduces a culture, people, or identity to an emaciated version of itself. For BIPOC in your congregation, these curricula offer only a fragment of their culture and are often not healthy or accurate. To speak about BIPOC cultures as inherently violent or inferior is to affirm the notion of White superiority.

Some curricula do not provide any expression of BIPOC and non-Western culture, featuring all White faces and perspectives. Instead, they ask Black and Brown congregants to divest from their own cultural and racial identity to be formed by material steeped in White pseudosupremacy. For example, it is a very White approach to describe sin exclusively as a series of actions or thinking patterns found in an individual: don't lust, don't be greedy, don't curse. Sin exists on a structural and corporate level as well. The work of the gospel addresses not just our individual sinfulness but also structural sin. We emaciate the impact of the incarnation and resurrection by focusing only on an individual's sin. Structural racism, imperialism, and colonialism are sinful too, and Jesus can redeem us collectively from them! Ensure that your theology on sin and redemption are expansive enough to talk about racism and anti-racism.

One thing I look for when pursuing curricula is if the material is explicitly anti-racist. Over the last few years, a torrent of justice-minded books and content have been made available for churches. But not all this content is interested in racial equity; some of it instead tries to foster diversity without addressing White pseudosupremacy. I also seek out a curriculum that can consider the experiences of others across racial, class, and sexual identities. Avoiding the erasure of these identities is crucial for our spiritual formation and capacity to be in solidarity with vulnerable communities. Curriculum creators and authors willing to be intentional about equity inclusion will avoid many of the pitfalls of the problematic content highlighted above.

DECENTERING OURSELVES

Another truth about small-group formation tends to get White people all up in arms, but if we truly desire to be existentially anti-racist, it's a truth we would do well to accept: sometimes, BIPOC need BIPOC-only spaces. Now, I'm not promoting segregation, so stop freaking out. And also, miss me with the "but that's racist against White people" fabrications. Whiteness is *everywhere* and even the nicest of us can be utterly exhausting to the BIPOC community: just because we know we're nice people doesn't mean *they* do, and so a lot of their energy goes toward being ready for the racist ax to fall. Many of my Black friends have told me, for example, that they'd rather stand in a room with a man in a white hood and cape than with a White liberal progressive like me, because at least with the guy in the white sheet, they know where they stand. That means that my very embodiment can feel dangerous to people of color, and if I really care more about these people I cherish than I do about my feelings, I'm going to honor the fact that sometimes, they just need to be away from me and my glaring Whiteness. And that really is OK. Shockingly and for reasons I can't explain, they still love me, and I honor both their Blackness (or other identities) and their humanity when I do this gracefully. Offering a small-group option for BIPOC allows them power to choose what best serves their needs, and that's a very hospitable thing to do.

For those of us who are in primarily White churches, the work is about cultivating a space where we see and practice agency over our own Whiteness. Examining our curriculum, reading and interacting with voices of color, and learning from their experiences through the books and other media they produce are a great start to deconstructing our own racial identity as well as our small-group ecosystems. Most importantly, we need to cultivate brave spaces for Whiteness to be seen and healed. By this, I mean we need to create spaces in which it becomes a moral imperative to call out racist contexts when they happen, to examine the racist tendencies that our brains have used to categorize ourselves and each other, and to do the work of divesting ourselves of power and privilege whenever possible.

Before you ask, the answer is yes. It will cost you something, including money. Here's where the warm fuzzies often leave the anti-racist movement—as soon as the discussion moves to line items on the budget. Yes, divesting ourselves of power means we *in*vest time, energy, and money in things like anti-racism training for small-group leaders. It means you take and make time to do the messy work of telling the folks who have been leading for years that no, they can't lead another small group until they get trained, and no, we'll be using a different curriculum this year. And it includes responding to all the angry White emails you get when you explain that yes, you will be hosting a BIPOC-only group for those who might find that beneficial.

As we move into the question segment of this chapter, consider how your small groups are currently run, and how they may be agents for either empire or anti-racism for your congregants. Either way, your small groups will tell you a lot about how you're doing in the realm of your justice work, and they can be a place for real transformation in your organization and the people it serves.

ASSESSMENT 4.2: SMALL GROUPS

1. What sort of training do your small-group leaders get around anti-racism and White silence work? If they do not currently get training, how will you start and what tools will you give them?
2. Do you have a known process for BIPOC members to safely address instances of microaggressions if they feel unsafe in small groups?
3. Does your small-group curriculum support empire and supremacy culture, or does it promote a divestment of power?
4. In what ways might your small group resist becoming a clique? How can you encourage open welcome to radical difference?
5. Does your small group have a construct within which to talk about racial matters? Have you provided a lexicon and a framework for these conversations to happen in a healthy and constructive manner?
6. What metric exists to ensure your curriculum is shaped by voices outside of Whiteness and to pursue content with an **intersectional** approach to spiritual formation and community?
7. How does your congregation determine if the curriculum's objective pulls the group toward White middle-class norms or toward a more inclusive expression of God's kin-dom that values equity and belonging?
8. How can your congregation be intentional about listening to the voices and experiences of differently abled and queer believers? Regardless of your church's theological stances or practices, it is critical to listen to these voices.

5

Buildings and Grounds

I grew up in Dumont, New Jersey, on the land of the Lenape, but I had never even heard that name until I was in my mid-forties. I had no idea who the Lenape were, and I certainly never heard them remembered in school or at any public event or church service. There were other markers of our history: We had a war memorial that looked a little like a miniature Washington Monument at the far eastern edge of town, known either as "the monument" or "the circle," because it stood in the middle of a particular traffic configuration. There was the cemetery at the corner of Madison and Prospect that had graves older than the founding of the town, which was as recently as 1894, because the area was invaded by the Dutch before the Revolutionary War and for a long time was known as Shraalenburgh. But nowhere was there a remembrance of the original people native to that land. I didn't hear about them in school. I didn't see any monuments to their memory or land set aside for their honor. They had been effectively erased from history and therefore from my consciousness. The land's history was, as far as we were all concerned, a history of European Whiteness and American revolution.

The story of my hometown is an excellent example of how Whiteness renders the marginalized invisible, consumes the entirety of space, and then becomes invisible to itself through its presumed self-ascribed normalcy. But the history of place and the influence of its people are strong, and they still assert themselves in subtle ways we barely see.

81

There is also a certain power in a name, and this is how the Lenape still resonate in Bergen County, often unnoticed, in the legacy of the surrounding towns. A quick drive up or down Route 17 (actually, probably not so quick with the New Jersey traffic) will move through Ho-ho-kus and Hackensack, Paramus and Mahwah, where the voices of this ancient people might call out for recognition even through their anglicized, appropriated appellations.

There is power in the force of place and space, and yet place and space is one of the influences upon our psyches that goes the most unnoticed and underestimated. After all, the ground, we assume, will always be beneath our feet. The deeply complex connection of people to the land is such an important concept that it could probably be an entire book in itself. When we think of legacies like colonization and its violence, war and its power dynamics, and the history and genealogy of race in America, the power of place becomes even more important. When we combine all of that with a faith narrative, in a place where God is being named and recognized, the power of place can become holy and sacred and also something that renders deep harm. That's why it is so incredibly important to make sure we are working with the concept of place in a way that truly honors God, and to do that, we need to consider all who enter a place—past, present, future. There needs to be a paradigm shift away from the ownership of place and toward a stewardship of space: a sense not that "this place is ours" but that "we have been charged with caring for this sacred place so that all may enter its holiness."

Thinking about the space and place of church is both important and problematic. We know, of course, that "church" is really a misnomer when applied to a building. We are the church—you and I—and the brick-and-mortar structures we tend to gather in do not represent the body of Christ that we hope to love so well. But of course, we also know that buildings have very much become a part of our church culture, whether they are archaic, historical places deeply entrenched in history, or sparkling new edifices erected in this twenty-first century. In postpandemic times, the space and place of church is morphing into online screens, and it will be interesting to see what the long-term effects of this transition will be and how we will use our physical spaces differently, if at all. Still, it is an important endeavor to consider what our space says about who we are and what we stand for. It's also imperative to acknowledge and, when possible, repair any harm done by our occupation of space and place in history, in the present, and into a more responsible future.

Before we dive into the specifics of our own church buildings, we need to understand a little about what makes space and place so powerful. Why does it matter if we know who was here before us, how our sanctuary is arranged, what the front entranceway is like? It matters because space and place leave indelible markers in our psyches that forge us into who we are, what we believe about ourselves and each other, and they have a direct impact on how we behave.

THE POWER OF SPACE AND PLACE

Space and place hold power because they define us as much as we define them. Because the spaces we move through define us, they also define the way we act. When you are at home, for example, you are in a space that defines you as a resident—the space is yours, and you are most likely very powerful in that space. When you are at someone else's house, you are defined as a guest. Your defined role brings with it certain behaviors that are considered acceptable or not, depending on who you are in the space you are currently inhabiting. Public spaces have even more complicated rules that are often unspoken but somehow agreed upon nonetheless.

Space defines what is appropriate behavior based on your relationship to it, and we arrange ourselves in space depending on what identity the space assigns to us. To pull from our racist history, remember that Black people were arranged into the backs of buses, the back doors of coffee shops, and different restrooms for decades. This is a perfect example of how space perpetuates power and seeks to define some of us as more worthy or valuable than others, and also how space can be used by dominance to subjugate whomever it pleases.

There are other ways that behavior and power are defined by space. Who has access to a space, who is considered "in charge" of a place, who holds "ownership" are all ways of defining both identity and power. In turn, whoever holds power makes the rules and defines what behavior is accepted within the space. Consider, for example, that when you are at home, you are the "owner" of the space, and other people are your guests. The specific rules (and power) associated with those two identities will shift when you visit your friend's house, or when you're both in a restaurant.

When we begin to consider the way Whiteness operates in public spaces, we must consider all the ways that Whiteness holds dominance in the public sphere, and all the rules that go along with that. In *Good White Racist?*, I discussed the power of the racial contract—an unspoken social agreement that Whiteness has made with itself about Blackness that designates a certain social hierarchy:

> The purpose of the racial contract is really nothing more than self-maintenance. It's designed to benefit White people and to allow for the exploitation of BIPOC communities—their bodies (slavery), their land (think the American colonies and First Nations people), and their resources (consider the way South America has been raped for its natural resources).[1]

The important thing to remember here is that members of the BIPOC community don't agree to the racial contract; rather, it is "an agreement that *White people make with each other, over the non-White population.*"[2] Because Whiteness controls space and place, Whiteness has created norms for identity and behavior, and when you back that up with the power of God, well—things can get pretty dicey. Especially if all your imagery suggests that God is a White guy.

A light-skinned, blue-eyed White guy. With amazing abs, no less.

In Christian imagery, we have the holy male trinity of the proverbial White bearded old man, the buff young Jesus, and the White, cherubic boy born in a manger. (The actual third person of the Trinity, the Holy Spirit, is more often spoken of in feminine language, but she—of course—remains disembodied.) These images, from newborn son to virile young man to wise fatherly elder, have two things in common: Whiteness and maleness. They leave a whole lot of the rest of us moving through space feeling a bit less than, under the gaze of our stained-glass White Jesus and venerating the White male body as somehow closer to the Divine.

The point is, when we think about space and place as an institution (and a holy one, at that) we also have to start thinking about Whiteness. Because we recognize that power and place go hand in hand, it's a worthy endeavor to examine who is ascribed power in place and also who is rendered invisible by that power. Because when Whiteness takes over a space, it has a habit of making a whole lot of people really hard to see, even when they are right there in front of you. Case in point: I never knew about the Lenape even as I grew up surrounded by towns named in their language.

THE DEVASTATING EFFECTS OF WHITE "PROGRESS"

When Whiteness is in charge of powerful institutions such as government, real harm can come to those marginalized communities that Whiteness prefers not to see, and it can happen by the use and abuse of the power/space/place dynamic. A very real, very painful example of this is the way so many Black Wall Streets throughout the country have been decimated for the sake of White "progress," with devastating results for members of those communities that lasted for generations. Black Wall Streets were centers of Black economic power—thriving communities built around Black-owned businesses in which Black folk could succeed, build wealth, and keep that wealth within their own communities and families. Businesses grew, faith organizations flourished, and access to the so-called American dream was not blocked by the usual obstacles of systemic racism. These communities were self-sufficient and minding their own business, and they were thriving.

But when the institution of government needed to build a new highway or undertake some other sort of "urban development project," White communities were more highly valued and protected. Highways require place and space, after all, and it's certainly not the White church that will get torn down to make way. The highway would go directly through the Black communities, because these communities would not have the sort of social capital (i.e., friends in high places) to protect them and give them voice. Whiteness viewed these communities as "less than"—less important than, less safe than, less cohesive than—White communities, and therefore they could be dismantled in the interest of White-savior-driven reform.

The result was the dissolution of cohesive communities. In Hayti, North Carolina, where a highway was built through the community, creating a physical obstacle in the middle of the neighborhood, traffic to Black-owned businesses suddenly stopped. It became impossible to get to the supermarket, so not only did the supermarket go out of business, but the people who lived in the neighborhood had to travel longer distances to buy food, creating a **food desert.**[3] Food deserts are areas where it is difficult or impossible to find fresh, nutritious food. In the first decade of the twenty-first century, the US Department of Agriculture identified about 6,500 food deserts in the United States.[4] Food deserts intersect with other aspects of oppression; not only are they closely linked with high unemployment and poverty rates, but their populations also have higher rates of disease—and often less access to the health care needed to treat that disease. Because they live in poorer areas, public education is also underresourced and more difficult to access. And public transportation projects that would make it easier for the people in these communities to shop for food, see their doctor, or find a job are often nixed by White politicians who want to keep "those people" contained in their communities and out of the richer areas where—surprise—the White people live. Traveling farther to get food makes it more expensive—not only will it cost you more to get there, but the more time you spend traveling, the less time you have to work to earn money, much less have the luxury of disposable time—time spent dreaming, planning, or bettering oneself.

Here's what's so interesting about this cyclical system: it is a perfect example of how Whiteness literally creates poverty by destroying a community, then that community becomes a target for White church "ministry" and service projects. A White church that really wants to be anti-racist will not only work on the immediate need of feeding hungry bellies with nutritious and culturally relevant food (food that is familiar to and desired by the community they hope to serve); it will also use its influence and power to encourage government to fund public projects that eliminate food deserts and the other oppressive systems with which they intersect.

PLACE, THE WHITE CHURCH, AND GENTRIFICATION
(Bryana)

At first glance, place, the White church, and gentrification may not be intuitively connected. But together they create a dynamic that needs to be considered by all White churches attempting anti-racist work. **Gentrification** is "the restoration and upgrading of deteriorated urban property by middle-class or affluent people, often resulting in the displacement of lower-income people."[5]

To truly understand the harm done by gentrification, it is important to understand the historical context, which is often ignored, intentionally forgotten, or White-washed. The short version of the history lesson is this: there is a legacy of marginalization of BIPOC at the hands of White pseudosupremacy, including decades of **redlining,** which resulted in disinvestment from inner-city neighborhoods and a decrease in property values. This was further exacerbated by White flight, when White families fled urban neighborhoods as Black families moved in, because they were afraid their property values would plummet (thanks to redlining) and they would be integrated with Black people.[6] Therefore, property values in urban neighborhoods continued to plummet while suburbs flourished, perpetuating the racist belief that urban neighborhoods caused these issues, and the only way to fix them is for White folks (churches) to come in and "save" them, while never addressing the historical fact that this issue is a direct consequence of the injustices of White supremacy and systemic racism.

A deeper understanding of the historical context of these particular racist events dispels a common myth that poor BIPOC communities are poor because something is inherently wrong with them. These harmful narratives, such as "Black people are lazy," or "Black people aren't smart," or "Black people are more dangerous," or "Black people need saving," further perpetuate the myth that Black people are at fault for communities in inner cities being in disrepair. The truth is, Whiteness caused this. So, what does this have to do with White churches and anti-racist work? There are two important considerations.

First, if you are a faith leader considering a church plant in an urban area (or moving to one), I encourage you to get deep with what your intentions are for doing so. Following millennials and younger families into the cities to "revitalize an underserved community" may seem like a shiny object of opportunity for ministry, but please consider the harm this causes. While perhaps well intentioned, "revitalizing" an area forces out current residents (primarily BIPOC) as property values go up. This is happening nationwide to Black churches and other congregations of color. BIPOC are being forced out of their communities (where their churches are located) and pushed geographically farther from their church, which often forces them to find a new church community (because transportation costs money). Ultimately inner-city churches close, and it is likely a developer or a White congregation that will take "ownership" of the abandoned buildings and churches— leading to further divestment from BIPOC people and communities.

Second, it is also important to be aware of the **White-savior complex**—this mistaken idea that an urban ministry helps people who cannot help themselves. I'd like to take a moment to recognize the significance of the Black church, for example, as a space for Black folks to feel valued and connected with the Divine. The "Black Church is as diverse as it is foundational to the African American experience," says Henry Louis Gates.[7] In *The Souls of Black Folk* (1903), W. E. B. Du Bois writes, "One can see in the Negro church today, reproduced in microcosm, all the great world from which the Negro is cut off by color-prejudice and social condition. . . . Practically, a proscribed people must have a social Centre, and that Centre for this people is the Negro church."[8] Black churches were the first institutions built by Black people for the safety, security, and liberation of Black people. Gates writes:

> Rooted in the fundamental belief in equality between Black and white, human dignity, earthly and heavenly freedom, and sisterly and brotherly love, the Black Church and the religion practiced within its embrace acted as the engine driving social transformation in America, from the antebellum abolitionist movement through the various phases of the fight against Jim Crow, and now, in our current century, to Black Lives Matter.[9]

Leaders of preexisting predominantly White urban churches should consider supporting local Black churches and take the posture of learning from them. There is a wealth of knowledge and connection to the local communities in the Black church. Recognize and honor their value, and their local impact, which includes trusting and supporting these communities with no strings attached. For those considering an urban church plant, I encourage you to interrogate your true intentions behind that motivation. If you are planning an urban church plant in a community where there are already thriving churches (also interrogate the White pseudosupremacy in your definition of "thriving"), that in and of itself is gentrification. Consider the likely harm that will cause to the local communities.

One final consideration is for predominantly White congregations that are sharing a building with a BIPOC or multicultural faith community. It is not possible to share a space without church activities and missions intersecting; however, sharing a building with a BIPOC or multicultural faith community does not count as a multicultural/racial badge of honor for the predominantly White congregation to claim. Given our racist history and present, multiracial and multicultural churches can't thrive without naming and addressing the imbalance of systemic power and privilege within the four walls of the church. Ask yourself if this arrangement ensures the equitable participation of the BIPOC folks. Are they expected to assimilate? Do they have equitable representation at all levels of decision making? Sharing a building with a BIPOC faith community is not synonymous with having a multicultural faith community.

ASSESSMENT 5.1: CHURCH PLANTING
AND BUILDING-SHARING

Current Church Planters:

1. How did you assess the neighborhood or community you planted in? Did you take the presence of BIPOC into account?
2. Are you in a neighborhood that is experiencing gentrification and "renewal"? What inspired you to pick this particular location or church building?
3. Is anyone from the local community attending these new church plants?
4. Is your church plant supporting the gentrification of the local community or does it offer support to the local BIPOC leadership? If so, in what ways?

Those Considering a Church Plant:

1. Are there already churches in the community where you are considering a plant?
2. How might you consider supporting thriving church communities in ways beyond a church plant?
3. Do you have a good understanding of the needs of the local community, and how they have been or currently are being impacted by racist systemic policies, systems, and so on?

A Congregation That Shares Their Space
with a BIPOC Congregation:

1. Is your space a place of safety for the BIPOC congregation? Are you prioritizing safety in your buildings for the BIPOC members?
2. Is your space inclusive to the BIPOC members? Are they able to use signage and decorations and other cultural representations without the need for permission and without being chastised?
3. Does the BIPOC congregation have equitable access to resources, as well as any decision making involving the "place" or building?

4. Do you have the same level of standards for cleanliness and maintenance for all parts of your building, no matter who occupies them? Is the BIPOC congregation relegated to the "forgotten" areas of your building?
5. Do you have a shared (and equitable) covenant that outlines shared values and expectations regarding the sharing of the church?

YOUR ORGANIZATION'S USE OF PLACE AND SPACE

We've used the terms *space* and *place* somewhat interchangeably thus far, but I think it is important to define them more directly before we dive into a discussion of how they operate in our specific organizations. For our purposes here, **place** *relates to the local geography, community, and culture within which an organization exists, and the history pertaining to them.* For example, when we work to understand *place* we will look at the history and nature of the land and its ecologies, and how that impacts the culture of the area. We will look at the community and how our organization has interacted with it. And we might examine how the local culture impacts our organization and vice versa. **Space** *relates to distance, proximity, and access, and the power dynamics that result from the ways in which these are used in an organization.* An audit of the way space is used to perpetuate dominance, for example, might examine who is kept farthest from the center of power and access and for what reasons; we might wonder who has the most access and how that impacts their power and influence in the organization and in the community beyond. We might seek to understand the ways in which our space is assembled and constructed to perpetuate or dismantle these power structures.

Now that we understand a bit more about the power of place and space, we can begin to intentionally interrogate the ways in which they operate in our own organizations, and how we might want to do better. We can begin by understanding that Whiteness has a certain way of inhabiting place and organizing space.

Place

As institutions that hold a position of cultural, political, and spiritual authority, churches have a unique ability to perpetuate racist ideology by continuing to ignore the impacts of social institutions such as colonization and slavery, or to begin to resist pseudosupremacy by first naming its existence. Learn the history of the land on which your church building sits, and honor the pain and loss that may be part of that history. For example, recognizing as a regular practice that the very ground your building stands on is in reality a tribal land—that it is a place of ancestry and history that has nothing to do with Whiteness—is a good place to start. Or perhaps we can recognize that our building stands on what was once a plantation. We can ask ourselves about ways in which our church may have benefited from the enslavement of Black people—was it built by enslaved hands, or funded by families who enslaved people? We can work this remembrance into our liturgies, for example, in our opening prayers, our Communion tables (a time of deep and intentional re-membering), and our benedictions. But this type of work—while important—can easily become performative. It is imperative that we begin to bring into the White imagination the realities of past transgressions against BIPOC, but mere White imagining is not enough.

In order to be truly anti-racist, we must begin to do the hard work of divesting ourselves of power and privilege. We often resist this, because it requires us to reorganize our priorities. That reorganization hurts because things that have always felt important—and sometimes actually are important—suddenly need to take a backseat in the interest of rebalancing for the sake of true equity. It hurts because this work may require a redistribution of funds (and anti-racism efforts too often get sidelined as soon as they get too close to the purse). Let me put it this way: it's possible that you're totally fine with including a remembrance of the tribal peoples who inhabited the land on which your church building sits in your liturgy. But if I suggest that you seek out an organization that represents those people currently, and pay them a lump sum of back rent and commit to paying a monthly rental stipend for your use of their land, chances are you're already hyperventilating a bit.

I get it.

After all, you've got important things in your budget you have to pay for, and church budgets aren't all that big to begin with. But this is the difference between performative allyship and real anti-racism. Many White people balk at the idea of financial reparations such as this, often saying things like, "Oh, it's always all about the money." And I'm here to tell you that it's not *all* about the money, but it's *a lot* about the money—because money is one of the key tools that

Whiteness has used to keep BIPOC oppressed. We have decimated Black centers of business, we have profited off of enslaved labor, and we continue to pay BIPOC less money than White men for the same labor. How we use—and don't use—our money is a representation of our values, and as moral documents, our budgets can offer some painful insights into the truth of our organization's priorities. Our budgets can become real tools for our becoming anti-racist, if that's indeed what we want to become.

So yes. It's about the money.

It's also about people, and place impacts the identity of our congregation in very real ways. A church I was once deeply involved with started out in a small storefront space on Main Street, between a liquor store and a bar. The congregation was always diverse not just racially but also generationally and socioeconomically. There were, on any given Sunday, wealthy pro football players sitting next to people who experienced shelter instability or who were currently without a home. The church leadership, though, had always dreamed of building a big, shiny monolith on a hill. That vision succeeded, but the hill they built on was far from the center of town. In fact, it practically sat on the border of its wealthy neighboring municipality. Public transportation (for those who could afford it) to the area was limited, and foot traffic practically nonexistent. Within weeks, the congregation's identity shifted to a more homogeneous, solidly upper-middle-class population. Now, the only people we met experiencing shelter instability were the people we "served," and this changed the power dynamic significantly.

Space

We also need to think about the ways in which we use the space in and around our buildings. Does the placement of the altar and its sacredness create a sense of exclusivity—some idea that only certain people are worthy of coming close to God? Do we banish certain populations—children, nursing moms, the underbathed—to realms hidden and unseen, or do we welcome them in the fullness of their noise and mess? Do we consider their noise and mess somehow less holy and beautiful than our own noise and our own mess? Do we shuffle the shelter-insecure off our front steps in search of some sort of respectability? Do we use our building to keep people out or invite people in?

Another important point to address is safety. For example, I know of one church that was placed in a prime space to minister to people experiencing food and shelter instability and mental illness due to their proximity to numerous social services organizations, but they consistently moved these people off their front stairs because of the danger they believed these people posed to the preschool that was on-site, which was both an important ministry to the town and a primary source of income. Of course, the safety of children and families is of high priority—but it bears asking the question: why is their humanity more valued than those who are experiencing economic insecurity and mental illness? Here is a perfect example of how we might miss an opportunity for justice offered to us by place. A divestment of resources from, for example, a poorly designed voluntourism trip into a well-trained security team (and by "well-trained," I do *not* mean well armed) could help this church respond to the very human needs of all of these people—not just the dominant culture, but those on the margins as well.

Many of the rules of our space are hard to define because they are unwritten and unspoken—at least, in the ways we'd normally think of. Rather, the rules are shouted from the imagery that hangs in our buildings—like stained-glass windows of White Jesus—and reinforced with locked doors, territorial staff, and the proverbial side-eye from protective lay leaders. Power reverberates through the walls of the space as we refuse to allow cultural practices of Indigenous people to take place within them. For example, I once worked with an evangelical church with a large Mexican population that hoped to commemorate Día de los Muertos, the Day of the Dead. The holiday, popular with many people from Latin America, is a day of prayer and remembrance of the dead, but the White pastors of this church felt uneasy with the skull imagery and considered the practice too "witchy" and "pagan" to occur within church walls. Their refusal to honor this important part of their congregants' faith and culture demonstrated White dominance and ownership of space, not to mention a deep ignorance of the holiday and its meaning. Similarly, when we invite BIPOC into our sacred altar spaces only once a year, during Black History Month, to perform their Blackness for us with a nice gospel tune, we may feel as if we are sharing our space generously, but we are also using space to tokenize and commodify Blackness and its art, often with the result of having our Whiteness feel placated for how totally not White it's acting.

The concept of sacred profanity[10] helped me to have a paradigm shift that impacts how I think about liberation, about God, and about the systemic abuse of power, and I think it can be useful for us here as we think about our opportunities to engage with sacred profanity in our space and place of our church. Sacred profanity speaks to the idea that God is not so sanitized as to be above the most mundane, everyday aspect of our lives, and even the profane. I first heard the idea relative to hip-hop music as a defense against the genre's tendency toward violent and misogynistic imagery; the argument (and I think it's an excellent one) is that it is not hip-hop that is profane, but rather the systems of oppression that cause poverty, violence, addiction, and rage.

ACCESSIBILITY IN YOUR SANCTUARY

As we think about the ways in which space and place contribute to power dynamics, we must consider accessibility and people who are differently abled. One of the ways that power is perpetuated is through access: who has access, and who does not, reinforces power dynamics and inclusion in very real ways. Who gets to stand in the pulpit—and who doesn't—is about power. Who can access the altar and who can't (perhaps because of stairs or other physical obstacles) is about power. Unfortunately, buildings are often not designed with full access for all—including people whose mobility depends on wheels rather than feet—and therefore are inherently designed to support dominance. If your space needs ramps or other modifications to be fully accessible, that investment of resources should be nonnegotiable.

Additionally, when we think about the myriad of differences in sensory perception, we might realize that some people find the music we hold dear to be quite literally unbearable, or the lighting too harsh or stimulating, or the hard pew too much pressure on their body. Many churches offer personal amplification devices for those who are hard of hearing; consider what other items you might make available to help everyone feel comfortable in your worship space.

When we begin to reimagine a space that promotes true equity and accessibility for all, we start to see all the ways in which our spaces have been designed to keep people out and maintain power dynamics. It requires a true imaginative edge and a justice-oriented creativity to discern strategies to resist the way our buildings were built to perpetuate dominance.

Sacred profanity tells us that even in those moments when we are embroiled in the impacts of systemic oppression, even as we are playing our profane parts—whether that is the profanity of White pseudosupremacist complacency or of BIPOC gang violence in response to poverty—God meets us there, in that very moment, rendering that profanity sacred.

The way I have seen churches protect our spaces from sacred profanity is unsettling. I have seen people experiencing homelessness shooed away from church steps. I have seen those struggling with mental illness carefully silenced, quietly herded out the back door, so as to not disrupt the service. I have seen the drunk and the high turned away, their smell too visceral for our privileged nostrils to endure. I can't help but wonder about the systems of profanity that have created these realities, and how many opportunities to experience God we have missed by being overprotective of our buildings, our spaces, and our noses.

While I recognize that there are real consequences to getting into the trenches of this type of profanity—practical ones, like how your insurance rate might be impacted, and the complaints you'll get, and the possibility that you'll have to clean up some messes (both literally and figuratively)—I'm also here to remind us that Jesus is a blood-and-guts kind of God. He's the kind of God who heals us with spit and mud, not bleach and Lysol. He engaged those we might consider clinically insane and confronted the systems that kept them in chains. He got up close and personal with the wounds of the leper and remembered them into community. And he wasn't afraid of the smell when it was time to call Lazarus out of the grave. Jesus saw the profanities of life and dove in without hand sanitizer. If our spaces are bleached too clean for profanity, we might also be too White-washed to see Jesus there, too.

ASSESSMENT 5.2: PLACE AND SPACE

1. During your next worship service, look around. How are people arranging themselves in the space? Why do you think that is?
2. Who is excluded by the way your space, including your altar, is arranged?
3. Is your church space highly sanitized or does it make room for sacred profanity and human mess?
4. How can you use your space to create a more inclusive, more welcoming environment for everyone?

SEPARATE SPACES FOR BIPOC HEALING (JOSH)

For so long, I told myself I stayed in the congregation because of my conviction for racial justice. I was convinced I was advocating change for the love of God's kin-dom and the love of my neighbor. Maybe this was true; what I did know to be true is that I needed this church to change for me. I wanted nothing more than to help turn the church into a community where I belonged and was seen. It took a long time to become this vulnerable with myself and see that the driving force of my racial equity work was just to be safe to belong. This motivation is common for so many BIPOC doing the hard work of racial justice in congregational life. But this longing would only come to fruition if the White congregation would allow it. See, my vision of belonging and community was still reliant on White folks' whims and willingness to affirm my place in the order of things. My (our) liberation cannot be reliant on the hope of White folks waking up. I was near the edge of burnout when I realized this and discovered the Roots Project. Right at the edge of breaking apart and coming undone, my healing journey began.

The Roots Project began in Tampa, Florida, through the labor of Melyssa Cordero and Keisha Polonio. The Roots Project was an initiative to prioritize minority leadership development and racial healing within the context of a ministry they were part of in Tampa. I stumbled upon an incredible talk by Melyssa while searching for resources to help me avoid burnout as a BIPOC staff member at a White church and reached out to connect. She recognized the pain I was experiencing and related to the challenges of navigating White pseudosupremacy in predominantly White churches. She extended incredible hospitality and invited me to see the work of the Roots Project firsthand.

The Roots Project was structured like a class but felt more like a community. The group featured people with ethnic roots ranging from the global south and the Caribbean to the Middle East. Keisha and Melyssa were intentional in ensuring the needs of BIPOC came first, without concern for the inflammatory response of Whiteness trying to force its way into the experience. The Roots Project's beauty did not overshadow the inconvenient truth that it was birthed out of struggle. The group operated in an oppressive evangelical bubble, and Roots was their act of resistance and means of survival. Those who came to the Roots Project (myself included) came wounded.

White pseudosupremacy had nearly broken most of our spirits, and the group served as a deeply needed lifeline.

It was liberating to be in a space where the imagination, the future, and the vision from Black and Brown leaders mattered. This was what I needed to return home and cultivate, if not for the mutual aid of BIPOC, then for the sanctity of my mind and soul. The group gently pushed me to know who I came from and to go back and learn the stories and struggles of those who came before me. This push was my first step in the racial trauma journey and BIPOC healing.[11] They challenged me to carve out spaces where my Blackness would belong and invite others in with me. Doing so would take me to the next steps of the journey, holding a safe space to talk about race and racial storytelling.[12] I left Tampa charged up, no longer willing to try to thrive in oppressive White spaces. I would need to continue healing and genuinely invest in where I experienced belonging to avoid burning out and giving up.

NO, IT IS NOT SEGREGATION

One of the accusations leveled against the Roots Project and similar initiatives for BIPOC is that they perpetuate segregation. Since we understand historical segregation to be morally wrong, we sometimes hold the belief that these spaces reject unity in the body of Christ. Most White Christians would communicate something about unity, or that God did not intend the body of Christ to be separated by race. Some might even cite the Martin Luther King quote about Sunday being the "most segregated hour in America." Those sentiments have been used to launch diversity initiatives and multiethnic church plants designed to exemplify diversity but not designed to be anti-racist. The truth is, diversity under the boot of White pseudosupremacy is still just as harmful. The celebration of diversity over equity and the safety of BIPOC is telling in these spaces. They do not often empower BIPOC to create affinity groups to cultivate healing and belonging. Because of the popularity of these church movements and initiatives in the White church ethos, the idea of BIPOC creating exclusive space is generally viewed as divisive and restoring racial segregation.

We must rethink our response to these spaces if we are to dismantle White pseudosupremacy. First, we need to clarify what segregation is in order to not conflate BIPOC-exclusive spaces as a different side of the same coin. **Segregation** is the legal and enforced separation of races that subjugated Black Americans to subcitizen status. Segregation intended to keep the racial hierarchy and perpetuate White pseudosupremacy. This was done without the consent of Black Americans and enforced against their will. Integration that began in the 1950s was the legal end of segregation but was not enforced until well into the 1970s.

While it is a morally correct vision for America, one must understand that racial integration also destroyed many of the structures that sustained BIPOC communities. Just as BIPOC communities did not consent to legal segregation, there was no consent involved in how integration played out for these communities. Places that Black folks owned were largely wiped out, and the example Kerry offered about the North Carolina Black Wall Street was not an anomaly. Nearing the end of segregation, Black communities were kneecapped in cities like Detroit, San Francisco, and St. Louis through numerous policy decisions that undermined their ability to self-sustain. Policies included housing redlining, the placement of highways atop thriving Black business districts, and intentional divestment of public services that served Black folks. Before integration, Black communities that thrived had ecosystems that operated mostly apart from Jim and Jane Crow. Black folks managed their grocery stores, schools, medical clinics, financial institutions, and transportation services.[13] Black schools featured Black instructors teaching a curriculum that accurately portrayed Black history and culture.[14] Once integration began, the standardized curricula scrubbed much of this material for all students to learn from and leaned heavily on what was taught in segregated White schools, which was devoid of accurate teaching on Black culture, history, and the legacy of racism. This effort of erasure continues today with many states and communities seeking to ban content like the Pulitzer Prize–winning 1619 Project and resistance to teaching a more accurate history of racism.

Integration for BIPOC came at a high cost of losing so much of their (our) community. The protective buffers of BIPOC-exclusive spaces that offered safety from the toxicity of White pseudosupremacy began disappearing. The destruction of that buffer contributed to the disconnection from the culturally affirming community many BIPOC long for today. I came into existence on the other side of that social shift where interstate highways, the war on drugs, and intentional economic divestment had replaced much of the thriving ecosystems in Black communities. I found myself craving a space that would help me make sense of these historical traumas while finding affirmation in who the Divine created me to be.

The Roots Project was an oasis for me. I worked full time for an organization where I was not safe to push back on the ways White-ness operated. I turned around on the weekend and attended a predominantly White church where the same dynamic played out. I had no place to engage my anger or rage, no place to be affirmed or understood. It was exhausting and debilitating.

We must understand BIPOC-only spaces as necessary components for racial healing and identity formation despite preexisting narratives on racial unity and segregation. If you are a White reader and find yourself resistant to BIPOC-only spaces (and I know at least a few of you are), please understand there can be no racial equity or reconcili-ation without healing. These spaces are critical in that process. Social psychologists define it as normal and acceptable for humans to locate themselves in affinity groups for the sake of safety and connectivity. So, one must ask, why is there resistance to a very normal human behavior when BIPOC do it? One reason is that for most White folks, it is hard to imagine a space they cannot enter or are not allowed to go. That flies in the face of the racial contract and the conditioning of White pseudosu-premacy. However, to push against this conditioning and support the cultivation of these spaces is the work of the anti-racist. Congregations providing a physical place for these gatherings or no-strings-attached financial support are great ways to help protect these spaces.

ASSESSMENT 5.3: SUPPORTING BIPOC HEALING

1. For BIPOC in your community, what are the barriers to being connected to BIPOC-exclusive spaces?
2. What are the BIPOC-exclusive spaces in your community?
3. How does your congregation talk about racial unity?
4. How does your congregation prioritize BIPOC needs like heal-ing and empowerment *before* asking for unity from them?
5. What is your congregation doing to support the racial-trauma healing of BIPOC?

LET'S CHECK IN
(Bryana)

Phew! You have made it halfway through this book, and many hard truths have been shared so far. We have encouraged you to invest intentional time dedicated to introspection and reflection. How are you feeling? Is there tension in your body? It's important to recognize the physical impact of emotion.

Practicing mindfulness is a way to direct attention to your present experience and find ways to self-regulate. Being able to name experiences in the moment—for example, "As I read this chapter, I feel anxious in my body"—will actually help your body to relax. The body calms down when the mind recognizes what it is feeling. Can you name the specific feelings and emotions you feel? Perhaps defensiveness, guilt, or shame? I'm here to tell you that all of those feelings are predictable, because if we have spent a majority of our lives in the United States, we have been socialized into a culture of White dominance and pseudosupremacy. So if you're White, it's normal to be feeling defensive, because you've grown up in a society that centers and advantages White folks. You have the privilege of going through your entire life without uncovering the half-truths and untruths of your racial identity and the history of this country.

If you're a BIPOC, you may be feeling validated. Empowered. Or you may be feeling confusion and shame. After all, you, too, have grown up in a society that centers and advantages White folks at the cost of BIPOC. All of these feelings are normal.

I don't say that to let anyone off the hook. The critical piece of all of this is what you *do* with those thoughts and feelings. Do you push them down further until they are no longer in your consciousness? Do you lash out and remove yourself from spaces that continue to challenge you and bring up those unpleasant feelings? Or perhaps you practice gratitude for this gift of knowledge and truth and hold it. Just hold it. Process it. Interrogate it. And eventually you will *become*. Becoming isn't a destination. It's a recognition of the tremendous work we have to do, and the recognition that this is a *journey* to becoming, and we likely won't *arrive* in this lifetime.

Oftentimes, feelings of confusion, guilt, and defensiveness are fueled by a lack of knowledge and understanding of racism in America. As stated in previous chapters, those of us who have spent a majority of our lives in the United States have an individualistic perspective. This ideology likely has a lot to do with why, when we are first confronted with race and racism, we apply binary individualistic assumptions. In other words, *I believe myself to be a good person, and good people aren't racist. Therefore, there's no way I can be racist. That's for bad people.* And the dialogue ends there. What we often fail to recognize is that racism is **systemic**. While none of us are wholly responsible for building the foundational pillars of a racist system, we are responsible for challenging the system, dismantling the system, and avoiding further perpetuation of the harm that the system causes those who are marginalized.

Exercising our race-consciousness muscles to recognize when we are challenging racism and not further perpetuating racism is not easy, and sometimes we forget to invest time in body and mind care along the way. So I ask:

— What are you feeling in your body as you read about some of the changes you will need to make?
— What does resistance feel like in your body?
— What does defensiveness feel like in your body?
— What does guilt feel like in your body?

As you notice these feelings in your body, close your eyes and pay close attention to them. Take a few deep breaths and focus on sending the breath to the places in your body these emotions are showing up. Breathe into them, creating space and room in your body for the emotion to flow through you. Remember that emotions are like waves: they will come, and they will go. Let them roll through you and know that they do not need to control your response.

6

Communications

The huge entryway of the Riverside Church in the City of New York was brightly lit, with beautiful imagery and signage all around; it felt welcoming despite its intimidating size and its cold stone walls. The lighting, the signage, the welcoming atmosphere created an energy in the space that communicated vibrancy and life. Not only that—its entryway demonstrated that it was a place that was cared for by its people. And people seemed cared for, too, based on the images of them that abounded.

I was visiting the church during a class in seminary, and the Rev. Amy Butler was taking us on a private tour before we spent the next day and half learning from her. She spoke about how when she first arrived at the church, the entryway looked very different, more dreary Gothic castle than vibrant community. Lightbulbs were broken, signage out of date, and overall the place was gray and drab. Knowing the importance of first impressions, Amy said the entryway was one of the first changes she made when she arrived.

This moment was a lesson for me that I have recalled often since that day, and it makes an important point to hold as we begin to consider how we manage marketing and communications: *everything communicates*. Communication is not just the talking you do with your mouth or the words you write with your computer. Signage, your church bulletin, the colors on your website, the way you care for your buildings and grounds—all of it communicates something about your organization and the things you prioritize and value. A dreary, dull entranceway might communicate a less-than-vibrant community that is not so committed to its own health and vitality. It might also communicate a lack of welcome and inclusion. On the contrary, a brightly lit foyer that displays attention to detail communicates an ethos of care, concern, and welcome to a place that is healthy and thriving.

We already spoke about buildings and grounds in the previous chapter, so we won't talk much about it here, but it is important to remember that your building communicates just as much as your bulletin does, so we'll be interrogating some aspects of that in this chapter too. We'll identify all the ways in which communication happens in your church and go through each of them together to discern ways in which these segments of the communications and marketing plan may be perpetuating supremacy culture.

Your Logo

It's always a good idea to examine your logo to identify if and how it may be communicating supremacist ideology. It's important to recognize that certain styles of crosses are associated with groups who have dedicated themselves to White supremacy, and other imagery might appear in our logos that reinforces this idea. The United Methodist Church, for example, has recently begun to look at the message inadvertently communicated by its cross-and-flame imagery, which could be seen as resembling a burning cross.[1] It also recalls the disturbing truth that it was a Methodist preacher who revived the KKK in 1915.[2]

Other, subtle forms of supremacy can sneak into our logos. For example, many churches use images of their buildings in their logos, which is often a nod to the congregation's history and its place in the community. But this is *also* a nod to things like ownership of Indigenous land and/or land that was worked by Black people who were enslaved by White people. Any good logo will proudly declare our values, and one that is all about your building may be placing an emphasis on property ownership and wealth over people. As beloved as your church building may be, it might be time to reconsider making that a cornerstone of your marketing and communications plan.

Your Website

Your website is often one of the first things that potential members will see about you, and it also may be a primary method of communication with your current members and the community, so it's important that it represents your values appropriately. If a key value of yours is to be anti-racist, then your website needs to communicate that clearly. However, this is an area where many churches fall into tokenism, often because of misguided good intentions. In a desire to create and promote diversity, these churches will often place images of Black and Brown bodies all over their website, hoping to attract Black and Brown people to their Sunday morning services. You'll remember that diversity programs just for diversity's sake can still be incredibly racist; if your church is primarily White, it's important to remember that you can be a predominantly White church and be awesome and radically anti-racist all at the same time. Putting a Black person on your home page isn't what makes you anti-racist.

That said, it *is* important to combat the idea of Whiteness being normative and lift up Black beauty by including Black faces in our marketing collateral. This is true and good and beautiful, but when those Black faces are only being used to demonstrate Black beauty without actual Black bodies in our church buildings being invested with influence, access, power, and authority, then we are merely tokenizing Blackness to make us feel better and look politically correct. This is not as paradoxical as it seems. I am not telling you to stop using pictures of your Black congregants in your marketing collateral. I am telling you to make sure those Black congregants are offered full participation and collaboration in your congregation. I am telling you to make sure they are fully heard and seen and loved and appreciated for all of who they are, including every inch of their Blackness, and yes, to submit to their leadership in how to do that in ways that are beneficial and not harmful.

If you do not have BIPOC members, please do not use cheesy stock footage to make it look as if you do. If you do have members from the BIPOC community in your congregation, then it is certainly a great idea to give them visibility—but not *just* on your website. If you're going to make them visible on your website, they need to also be visible in your church—in meaningful leadership positions, on decision-making committees, in your liturgy. Their culture and practices and music should be included in your services (not just during Black

History Month, by the way)—and led by them. However, this needs to be balanced very carefully so as not to overburden these families with requests to serve just to check a box on your anti-racism checklist. I can't imagine how draining it must be for BIPOC families to be asked to be in every photo shoot and on every committee because they're some of the few melanated members you have. Here is where authentic, organic relationship becomes extremely important. The deeper your relationship with these people, the more you can honor their emotional and energetic desire and capacity to lead.

Your website is also a place in which full transparency is absolutely required. If you're not a church that openly affirms and includes the LGBTQ+ community, say so. If a woman who is Black and gay walks through your doors, she deserves to understand exactly what will greet her when she gets there. It's innately cruel to state on your website that all people are welcome at your church when really what you mean is that they are welcome to attend services and tithe their 10 percent, but not to participate fully in sacraments like baptism or Communion, lead Sunday school, or get married by your pastor. It's *especially* cruel when your secret motivation is to forge relationship with them so you can "pray the gay out of them." People come to church seeking community and relationship with God and with others. To say you affirm her Blackness (not, by the way, that she needs your affirmation of her Blackness, or any part of her for that matter) but not her gender or her sexuality is straight-up mean, especially because the truth often comes out long after she has already invested time, energy, and emotion into the relationships she has developed there. This is a form of spiritual abuse. Please be clear on your website about who you are and what you believe so that prospective members can decide if they can find true belonging there.

Your Outdoor Signage

Your outdoor signage is another way that you communicate your values to the world. A church in my area was one of the very first churches to hang a huge—and I do mean *huge*—rainbow flag on their building, clearly communicating that they are fully affirming of the LGBTQ+ community. The result has been that families travel from almost an hour away to be part of this community where it is crystal-clear that they will be welcomed and affirmed. At another church I know, their

Black Lives Matter sign has been vandalized multiple times. Each time, they replace it, demonstrating a public consistency to their moral ethos and their commitment to the cause of anti-racism, even in the face of disconcerting criminal behavior by their neighbors.

Your outdoor signage should tell the story of what happens on the inside of your congregation. Quite often the White churches I work with experience conflict in their ranks about whether to place a Black Lives Matter sign on their building because they believe it's "too political." They seem to see those words not as a statement of human worth and value, but rather as indicative of a political organization, and they like to keep their politics and their religion separate. While I could write an entire book about how the Bible itself is a book of political resistance that demands justice for the marginalized, let's just say that your signage represents a chance to publicly declare which gospel you preach in the pulpit. As my pastor, the Rev. Ann Ralosky, says, "I don't preach politics, I preach the gospel. And when the gospel preaches politics, I preach the gospel."

Written and Spoken Announcements

There are a number of small ways that your church communicates either pseudosupremacist culture or an ethos of anti-racism, and many (though not all) are silent. Your bulletin is a place where you can clearly and consistently declare your stance on justice. Your mission and vision statement can and should be clearly marked here, and perhaps a statement specifically about racial justice would be apropos. But it's not just what you claim; your bulletin is often a printed (or perhaps digital) statement of what you *do*. It's a great place to go through a quick audit of your church's activities. What books have your small groups or book clubs been reading? Who leads your group activities? What service projects are you engaging in? All of these tell a story about who your church is and what it values, reinforcing those values to existing members and communicating them to newcomers in subtle yet powerful ways.

Your announcements are also an opportunity to express your anti-racist stance or to reinforce supremacist culture. It's not just about what's being announced—it's also about who is doing the talking, how they are saying it, and where they're saying it from. Your announcements are a time in your service in which you can both vocalize and display your values through your messaging and the body that delivers it.

Your Entryway and Greeters

Step outside your building, close your eyes for a moment, then step back in and ask what it is communicating. Does it tell the story of a congregation that cares for people? Does it communicate vitality and health or dysfunction and disorganization? Does it represent a warm welcome to everyone—and is that warm welcome actually true? When a new person enters your building, do they immediately know that you stand for anti-racism, or is it not a real priority for you that they know this?

It's also important to ask yourself, who is at the front of your building greeting people, what does that communicate, and is the message consistent and true? For churches with some diversity, too often I've seen members of the BIPOC community placed in highly visible positions—such as Sunday morning greeters—without being given actual influence within the organization. In other words, their bodies are used to communicate a diversity that's not entirely true, because a *truly* diverse organization includes influence from diverse sources in leadership positions. If there are no BIPOC leaders in your organization, then it's not diverse, it's oriented toward assimilation.

There's another subtle way that Whiteness happens in the entryway—especially among well-meaning White people who long for the diversity of the beloved community in a predominantly White church. Honestly, I feel awkward even trying to describe it—but it's this weird thing we White people do to try to demonstrate how incredibly happy we are that there are some Black people in the room. We act *super* friendly. We smile a lot. We are *really, really* nice. Because we want all the Black people to know how good and totally not racist we are. Dear God in heaven, sometimes we actually start trying to talk in African American Vernacular English.

It's cringey. It's awkward. It's straight-up weird, people. Just act like your regular self.

YOUR SOCIAL MEDIA AND PUBLIC ANNOUNCEMENTS
(Bryana)

Today we are more connected to each other than ever before, and there are good and bad consequences. If your church engages in social media, you probably already recognize this communication tool as an incredible way to reach current members and potential members with your mission, vision, and community activities. Before you leverage social media to communicate your church's commitment to anti-racist work, keep in mind the following five lessons:

Lesson 1. As a church, it is important that you take your social media content very seriously, especially when it comes to any messages regarding race, racism, and anti-racism.

Lesson 2. What matters in February matters year-round. Black history is American history. As one of the twentieth-century's greatest writers, James Baldwin wrote: "The past is all that makes the present coherent, and further, . . . the past will remain horrible for exactly as long as we refuse to assess it honestly."[3] The histories of Black accomplishments have often been minimized or erased throughout American history. While Black History Month is an opportunity to remember the great accomplishments of the African diaspora, there is another purpose: it holds the nation accountable to battling historical amnesia when it comes to the African American experience. Black History Month carves out a space for the African diaspora to be inspired and uplifted through stories and experiences of resilience. It is also an opportunity for White people to confront the nation's history of racism and to understand the ways it systematically (and individually) shows up today. With that said, it is important to recognize the performative nature of Black History Month social media posts. Find ways to celebrate African American history, and the contributions of Black leaders, throughout the year. It is also important to be mindful that your social media posts do not White-wash the critical work of historical civil rights activists. For example, we see political leaders today using the Rev. Dr. Martin Luther King Jr.'s words out of context to justify banning teaching about racism in US schools. Another less obvious example is avoiding messages challenging racial injustice in your posts, but rather sticking to "safe" posts of famous civil rights leaders' quotes.

Lesson 3. It's important that your social media feed doesn't just highlight the "good" your church is doing. Anti-racist work requires that you deconstruct the institution of Whiteness that upholds your church values. Anti-racist work requires that you openly name the systemic nature of racism and call out the ways your own church perpetuates the oppression of BIPOC. For example, if members of your specific church enslaved Africans and African Americans, create a public statement of repentance: "We at [Church Name] repent of our heritage of hate." There may be times when your church has perpetuated racism in the present day, which requires truth-telling in social media. For example, "We confess, as a predominantly White congregation, our use of a gospel choir last month without honoring African American history and culture outside of that particular Sunday is tokenizing. We need to do better."

Lesson 4. Carefully consider your public statements in response to racial violence. As a multiracial Black woman, one of the most harmful experiences I have had (repeatedly) in a church community is when the (White) pastor will acknowledge the tragedy (yet *another* innocent Black man lynched by a police officer) from the pulpit and be praised for being progressive just for acknowledging it. And that's it. Nothing else. Crickets. No acknowledgment of the trauma that this causes the BIPOC in his congregation, and more importantly the community. No call to action or direct challenge to the White congregation to care about this beyond the thirty seconds of acknowledgment from the pulpit. Equally harmful is when a public statement in response to a national racial crisis is constructed without engaging BIPOC leaders ahead of time. This is particularly important for churches who engage with BIPOC in creating a more racially conscious congregation. Don't mistake BIPOC engagement with an expectation that BIPOC will do the work or write the response. I specifically mean alerting them of the plan, giving them an opportunity to weigh in, and then trusting their contribution.

Lesson 5. Know when a public statement is unnecessary. We discuss throughout this book the ways to not only perform anti-racism but to authentically engage in anti-racist work. My challenge to all church leaders engaged in this work is to *do it without announcing it*. If you are early in the process, and have a lot of work to do, discern the appropriate time in your anti-racist journey to speak about it publicly. Whiteness has a tendency to confuse verbal commitment to anti-racist work with authentic action that is anti-racist.

ASSESSMENT 6.1: PUBLIC ANNOUNCEMENTS

1. Do you have a content plan that includes messages both honoring BIPOC folks and speaking truth about other systemic work that is still required to dismantle racism? Are you doing this during every month of the year, and not just during Black History Month?

2. Are you making public declarations of a commitment to anti-racist work in your church and surrounding community? If so, are you *living* that out in an authentic way? Authentic means not in a performative, White-savior way, such as posting pictures of international mission trips, or volunteering at a local food bank as a way of helping those in need.

3. Do you have a tragedy-response team that is equipped to respond to national tragedies involving BIPOC? Are you leveraging social media to appropriately respond to these national tragedies in both symbolic and tangible ways?

4. Is your social media manager (and/or volunteers designated to create social media content) equipped to manage messages about race, racism, and anti-racism? If not, how can you equip those people to do so responsibly?

EVERYTHING COMMUNICATES

All of these areas communicate what an organization values and prioritizes. Churches who desire to become truly anti-racist (and not just perform anti-racism) need to think about all of the ways we communicate and what we are saying when we do. I can't tell you how many times I have worked with church leaders who think the job is done when they put a Black Lives Matter sign on the front of the building; they do not make internal changes or create actionable plans for resisting supremacy culture or divesting power.

Even worse are churches (or Christian events) that use Black and Brown bodies to communicate an anti-racist ethos by placing them in visible positions in their marketing, but don't actually invest any power in those people—keeping them on display but not authorizing them with any influence in the organization. A perfect example of this is what happened to Ekemini Uwan at the Sparrow Conference in 2019. Though her presence as a speaker was actively promoted by the producers of the event, her talk—which called out racism and pseudosupremacy—was actively silenced, removed from recordings of the event and social media feeds.[4] Uwan had to hire a lawyer to obtain images and recordings of her appearance at the conference, which had used her embodiment to sell tickets, but was not willing to enter into any real self-examination of its own Whiteness.[5]

Predominantly White churches do something similar when we take tons of pictures of the one Black family and post them *everywhere* to make it seem as though we are a more diverse congregation than we actually are, while we decidedly resist doing any of the internal work we need to do to become truly anti-racist. This comes from the inaccurate belief that diversity is the automatic equivalent of anti-racism, and nothing could be further from the truth.

HOW COLORISM COMMUNICATES WHITE PSEUDOSUPREMACY (JOSH)

As Kerry mentioned, "everything communicates," and in our racialized world, the things being communicated are not race neutral. We've already named some explicit examples, like a large sign at a church declaring "Black Lives Matter." There is also a world of messaging that happens in more implicit ways below our consciousness's surface. To get to the roots of White pseudosupremacy, we need to dig deep and tear down some of the specific narratives that get communicated.

One of the most pernicious messages at play in our world is assigning value to BIPOC based on their proximity to Whiteness; this is the foundation of **colorism** and light-skin privilege. Beneath the preference for and selection of people with lighter skin or physical features that resemble European ethnic heritage is the underlying theme of "White is right," and those who can be closest to it are more proximate to rightness and goodness. This message is everywhere and extends well beyond the context of the United States. We can see it in cosmetics, where the global skin-lightening industry was worth an estimated $8.6 billion in 2020.[6] Asians and Africans seek to lighten their skin to achieve beauty standards defined by their closeness to Whiteness.[7] *Lighter is better* is a message that has been projected onto BIPOC for centuries, and that message has become internalized, shaping our capacity for self-love and disconnecting us from our cultural identity. Hollywood has shifted casting to appease specific international audiences that prefer to see lighter-skinned actors and actresses in films.[8]

In 2018 Heineken sparked controversy with an advertisement for its new light beer. In this ad, a bartender slides a beer to a patron who is out of the shot. Each scene shows the beer sliding past different patrons, most of whom are dark-skinned Black folks. The beer arrives in front of a lighter-skinned woman of color as the words "Sometimes, lighter is better" flash on the screen. The obvious message of colorism was inserted to help drive home the point about the light beer, but the backlash from the ad resulted in it getting pulled, and rightfully so.[9] Advertisements like this are by no means an anomaly; every year, advertisers and corporations get caught practicing colorism.

Colorism is deeply entrenched in our culture and has deep historical roots in the United States. Lighter-skinned enslaved Black folks were typically relegated to less arduous and physically demanding tasks and given higher positions in the plantation hierarchy. This often was due to their biological connection to the slave master whose rape of enslaved women resulted in pregnancy. Because of their White lineage, the child *might* be spared some of the more horrible abuses of chattel slavery. This historical trauma still lingers, and modern colorism is the fruit of this wound. Colorism assigns values such as beauty, kindness, and intelligence to lighter-skinned BIPOC while giving negative connotations to darker-skinned people (think of the beer commercial).

This even shows up in theology with how we talk about darkness and light. This valuing of lightness over darkness goes well beyond metaphors and has visceral effects. The messaging of colorism negatively impacts BIPOC and our ability to love how God made us. Churches must be careful not to participate in perpetuating these messages. Within congregational life, some of what we communicate likely upholds notions of colorism. In our theology, we must interrogate how we talk about aspects of darkness and light. Churches often conflate darkness with evil or sin and light with goodness and holiness. But God is still holy and beautiful in the darkness.

If we are only placing lighter-skinned or passing (appearing as racially White) people in positions of visibility and ignoring the presence of darker-skinned folks, what message are we sending? It is vital to remember colorism is about proximity to Whiteness, and churches often center the experiences of BIPOC who may not be lighter skinned but are in interracial marriages or are transracial adoptees. BIPOC persons in those categories have stories that matter and deserve to be told, but far too often, their stories are shared because they have proximity to Whiteness. Churches have a great deal of work to investigate if they value certain BIPOC voices over other BIPOC because of their proximity to Whiteness. We can begin the process by assessing which BIPOC in our congregation get visibility, influence, and leadership, and why. An unconscious bias of colorism may be undermining anti-racist efforts.

ASSESSMENT 6.2: COLORISM

1. If you're BIPOC, what messages were told to you about lighter-skinned BIPOC? What messages might you be internalizing about your beauty, intelligence, and value?
2. For BIPOC readers, what practices do you have to affirm your beauty and value? How are you reminding yourself you are made as God intended and all of you is beloved?
3. How might your church begin to enlist and empower voices who may not have proximity to Whiteness?
4. How has your church empowered voices of BIPOC in your congregation who may not share proximity to Whiteness?

ASSESSMENT 6.3: COMMUNICATIONS

1. Take a look at your church's logo. What does it communicate? Does the imagery perpetuate the dominance of land ownership through an image of your building?
2. Does your website clearly communicate your stance on anti-racism, both verbally and in pictures?
3. Do the pictures on your website and print collateral include stock photos of BIPOC or BIPOC who are not members of your church?
4. What does a review of your bulletin tell you regarding pseudo-supremacy or anti-racism in your church's activities?
5. Does your entryway communicate radical welcome for all?
6. Does your outdoor signage clearly communicate your anti-racist stance or does it participate in silence, complicity, and peacekeeping?
7. Who is made comfortable by your communications plan? Who is made uncomfortable?

7

Missions and Service

There is a deeply problematic paradox within the Christian missions–industrial complex: it is an institution of Whiteness that seeks to solve the problems Whiteness causes. The systems of racist poverty and suffering that have been caused by European colonialism all over the world are myriad and seemingly impossible to dismantle, but in order to begin to do that work, it's important for us to understand where the problems we hope to solve with our service and missions projects actually come from. To do that, Bry is going to introduce a guiding concept called the Groundwater metaphor.

THE GROUNDWATER METAPHOR

(Bryana)

The Racial Equity Institute, based in Greensboro, North Carolina, developed the Groundwater metaphor to explain that we live in a racially structured society that causes racial inequity. (Side note: I highly recommend REI's training. It's in high demand, and it will blow your mind.) The Groundwater metaphor was first inspired by Dr. Camara Phyllis Jones's insights in 2013.[1]

It's based on a simple tale of dying fish; essentially, the metaphor states that when you find a dead fish in a lake, you analyze the fish. Was it sick? If we apply the theory to the education system, for example, the fish is a single student, and we might ask questions such as, did it study hard enough? If you find half the fish are floating belly up in that same lake, you analyze the lake. In our educational example, we might try to ascertain how the system is failing and delivering the same unacceptable outcomes for half the students. If, however, we find that half the fish are dying in multiple lakes in the region, then we have to look at the groundwater. Because even though those lakes don't appear to be linked or connected, they are fed by the same contamination. Our job is to find the contaminant.

INHERENTLY RACIST COMMUNITY SERVICE

I spent five years on staff at a large, nondenominational evangelical church in New Jersey where I oversaw volunteers and community service, and though we did a lot of really good work, I see now that much of my good work was inherently racist. In order to explain, I have to tell you about the Newark YMCA.

When the Newark Y received a grant to bus at-risk youth from nearby Jersey City to their facility during after-school hours, it was an amazing opportunity for our church to develop a mentoring program in which we would match kids with congregants, then create opportunities for them to spend time together doing meaningful activities and forging relationships. In many ways, I am proud of the work we did there. We worked hard to build relationships with kids whose circumstances were incredibly difficult. We created systems to reduce harm, we had passionate mentors who really cared and wanted to do good. Our mentor-mentee matching system was in-depth and comprehensive. But overall, it was an exercise in White saviorism, because our church often felt great about the work we did there—and proudly paraded the program in front of congregants during weekly announcements—but never once tried to address the systems that caused those kids to experience the kind of poverty they did.

When I started the program, I was vastly naive and filled with good intentions that were not just incredibly misguided—they were also harmful. It wasn't until I started eating pizza with these kids that I began to understand the vast difference between my life and theirs. The point was driven home for me one day when one of them said to me, exasperated, "Look, I don't want to be in a gang, OK? But my mother has been dressing me in colors since I was a baby, so what am

I supposed to do?" I confess I spent a few days hating on that mother, judging her and thinking horrible thoughts about what she had done to her boy, until I realized that in actuality, she had done the most maternal thing possible: she dressed her baby in colors that she knew would keep him safe in the war zone that was her community. It took a few more years for me to realize that the war zone that this mother and child lived in was the creation of White pseudosupremacy, racist policies like gerrymandering and redlining, and a huge disparity in the ways these communities were policed and (under)resourced.

Meeting those kids and speaking with them helped me understand that my Whiteness does not know everything—including how to "save" those kids. In fact, my Whiteness does not really know anything about what it means to be Black or poor in America. The lives these kids live in Jersey City, just a few miles from my home, are a world away from the one my kids live. My kids can focus on flourishing because their basic needs—and quite a few supplemental desires—are met. The kids in my program, however, needed to focus on survival. They had a worldview that only consisted of the four-block radius they walked if they happened to go to school, and that walk was rife with both danger and an opportunity for them to put food on their tables with their street businesses. (Honestly, these kids understood profit and loss, cost of goods sold, and market value better than a lot of people I've met. We had a lot of conversations about it!) These kids also didn't expect to live past the age of eighteen, and so a lot of our work with them was designed to expand their worldview and their expectations of what was possible for them. If they couldn't see it, they didn't have a chance of making it happen for themselves.

Ultimately, our program was a huge failure, but not for lack of good intentions. Although we may have impacted a few lives for the better momentarily (and I like to hope that in some ways maybe we did) overall it failed because Whiteness—my Whiteness, my church's Whiteness (despite our well-documented diversity)—thought we knew best what these kids needed. While it's true that these kids did need tutoring and interaction with adults who cared about them, and while they really did benefit from having their worldview expanded, the truth is that at the end of their fourteen weeks in the program, they still landed right back on the impoverished street corner they came from. Their refrigerators would still be empty, and their best bet for staying safe and fed would be membership in a gang. Our work may have done some temporary good—and it definitely made us feel great about ourselves—but ultimately, it did very little to initiate real change in these kids' lives, because it didn't address the structural foundations of racism and poverty.

My leadership partner in this program was a Black man, and many Black mentors participated. But the fact is, the program was run by a church that held a White-dominant worldview. We were vastly under-resourced as a program. Whiteness tends to require "bootstrapping" of certain programs because it has other uses for its money, like big buildings and well-decorated corner offices. If such programs show a modicum of success, they are praised for their tenacious grittiness and get 'er done attitude. If they fail, they are lamented for not meeting some arbitrary bar of excellence that was most likely moved every time they came close to it.

We managed to accomplish a lot of stuff that made us feel good but, again, did nothing to actually change the systems that caused these kids to suffer. Changes to the system would require mass political advocacy that would go against the doctrine of unity that is so well wielded in evangelical churches to silence those who speak out for justice, naming us *divisive*. Ultimately, the only real success the mentor program could claim was a badge of honor for the church. On the other hand, it was a pivotal moment for me in my own spiritual growth and in the deconstruction of my own privilege in all its forms.

The mentoring program made me feel like a really good White person, and it also opened my eyes to my own privilege in ways I never expected. Even all these years later, as I reflect upon the experience, I learn more and more about my own Whiteness and how it plays out in my desire to serve the world. The problem here, however, is that White people tend to have our worldviews expanded by curated experiences that really do nothing to serve the communities we visit. The concept of **voluntourism** is a great example of this.

DEFUND SHORT-TERM MISSION TRIPS
(Josh)

We had already been to the site in our city too many times. We wanted to try somewhere new.

There weren't any openings at the other sites we wanted to travel to.

We want to love on the city.

This site was closest for us.

I want to make a difference.

The whole summer I worked for a Christian service-learning organization, I heard phrases like this from parents and students when I asked why they came to Philadelphia. Organizations like ours send students to sites around the country, from small rural communities to Native American reservations and large urban centers. Like most stated missions of service-learning organizations, the model impacts volunteers, which translates into impacted communities. But the reality of these experiences is far from a positive community impact.

Groups would sometimes pay upwards of $20,000 to travel to Philly and volunteer for the week. Their tasks ranged from sorting clothes at a Gospel Mission Shelter to picking weeds out of an abandoned lot that would become a community garden. These activities in and of themselves were relatively harmless. The actual harm came from the investment of time and money from youth groups believing their presence alone would make a difference in the community. That money would facilitate an experience for White suburban churches, but the communities they visit do not see or experience the impact of such an investment.

The lie of White saviorism has generated an entire industry of service-trip organizations for Christians to help poor (usually BIPOC) communities through an experience commonly called voluntourism. Students and their parents are sold a vision that their participation will generate meaningful change for a community. At the root of White saviorism lies the belief that White people can fix vulnerable communities' problems. These organizations capitalize on this lie by using terms like *partnership, collaboration,* and *sustainability* to sell it—and to be fair, they sell it well.

I was surprised and encouraged by the number of Black staff the organization had recruited, and nearly all of us were under the impression there would be authentic community collaboration and partnership. Those expectations would disappear for most of the BIPOC staff by the end of orientation. BIPOC staff experienced microaggressions from colleagues and leaders constantly throughout the training. I vividly remember phrases or statements shared during the training sessions that caused a visceral reaction from the staff of color. I witnessed their bodies tense up, yet I did not know what exactly had been said or done wrong at the moment. I was still coming into consciousness and believed in the mission and model of this organization. My naivete to the narrative of White saviorism led me to believe that our site could be different from other short-term mission experiences.

My site director, Dasha Saintremy, thought differently. Dasha is a Black woman who is gifted and driven as a leader and was the midwife for my own liberation, which started that summer. She had recently graduated from Interdenominational Seminary, where her training equipped her to call out White supremacy with ease. She had no patience for the White foolishness we experienced that summer and she helped pull the scales off my eyes to see the harm White saviorism was causing.

"When we gathered together and met our team for staff orientation, I realized how problematic things would be," she said when I asked her when she first noticed Whiteness at play in the organization. "All the Black staff leaders were seminary trained and had some type of outside leadership experience; the White staff leaders all had fewer qualifications but were given the same jobs. Once we got to our site, the White groups that would come to serve were shocked by my Blackness and disregarded me as the leader. The majority of the time, I second-guessed myself in leadership and felt like I had to show up differently for fear of being seen as the angry Black woman. Not only that, White folks would often come in and try to do things their way, even though the organizations and leaders we partnered with in the Philly community had their own system of doing things."

These organizations and the models they create do not lead to sustainable community change and are not suited to interrupt systems of White supremacy. I asked Dasha how these organizations and the churches supporting them can better use available resources to help BIPOC communities. She told me point-blank, "Organizations like these capitalize on the disenfranchised, disinherited, and marginalized. They say they're providing aid to a community, but they are profiting off those who lack resources and gaining resources from those who do have them. These organizations should cease to exist. If you want to help, give the money straight to the [BIPOC] organization doing the work on the ground. Allow them to make a system that works for them, fully and with no control."

The short-term mission-industrial complex makes White people feel good about their service, without considering whether it actually helped the BIPOC communities they served. There is a place for *local* service, but it must happen apart from centering the experiences, needs, and expectations of White volunteers. Real community change does not occur in a short-term context. We must let go of the idea that the presence of White people and their good intentions inherently leave a positive impact.

We must interrogate how we use terms like *partnership* and *empowerment* when thinking about service and missions. Partnership necessitates mutuality, and empowerment requires an intentional divestment from power to allow the other party to exercise theirs. These terms and others like them are often a cover to hold **paternalistic** and racist relationships with a BIPOC organization or community. The paternalistic mind-set in White churches and ministry organizations gives a false sense of dominance over the communities they seek to serve. These same churches and organizations often believe themselves to judge what is best for BIPOC communities. This strips BIPOC communities of the agency to consent in how they are served or resourced. Consent and agency are requirements to relationships that are rooted in mutuality and are the backbone of empowerment.

MISSIONAL PARADIGM SHIFTS

In order for us to participate in service projects that are not inherently racist, we need to embrace a few paradigm shifts that will change the way we look at our engagement with the communities we hope to serve. As we discuss these paradigm shifts, remember that they apply to both local service projects as well as international missions projects. Whiteness has had a global impact, so whether we're talking about a service project a few towns away or on another continent, the same theories apply—and so do the paradigm shifts we need to make.

Paradigm shifts like these get to the crux of the matter; they shift the very foundations of our thinking, which leads to changed behavior. When it comes to service and missions, we need to understand that (1) White saviorism perpetuates oppressive systems in order to serve Whiteness; (2) Whiteness does not know everything; (3) it's not just possible, but actually probable, that your congregation has needs that can be met and served by BIPOC communities. (This last one gets uncomfortable because it flips the hierarchy Whiteness holds dear, while also pointing back to that uncomfortable truth that White people enslaved Black people.) Let's unpack.

1. White Saviorism Perpetuates Oppressive Systems

When it comes to Christian service and missions, it's important to understand that it is, indeed, a self-perpetuating system. By this I mean that Whiteness has created an environment that resulted in poverty and dysfunction in BIPOC communities, then attempts to mitigate its own guilt by serving those communities. However, the services they provide only solve immediate and surface-level effects of a much deeper and systemic problem; the work does not challenge or dismantle systemic poverty and its cohorts, nor does it offer true repair. It simply helps everyone stay just satisfied enough to stave off revolt and maintain the status quo, and even this is with the barest necessities of survival.

The following diagram demonstrates the way White saviorism operates:

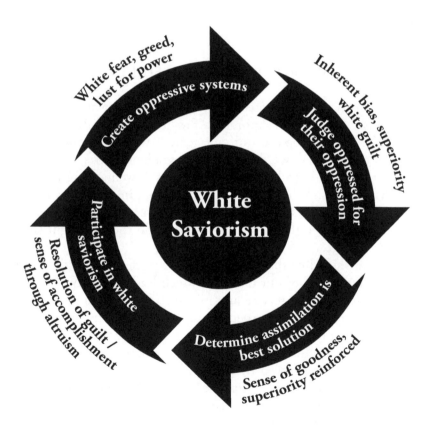

The Shift

An anti-racist seeks to disrupt racist systems, so when it comes to White saviorism, we need to go from being a player in the system to being a stick in the spokes. In other words, we need to disrupt the workings of the system. To do this, we need to go beyond the superficial needs— like feeding hungry bellies or passing out coats to people experiencing homelessness in the winter—and interrupt the core systemic issues, like politics, the distribution of wealth, and the management of resources. For example, rather than just creating soup kitchens in impoverished neighborhoods, we can also create foundations that help those neighborhoods thrive by listening to the community leaders tell us what they need and placing resources in their hands that will enable them to do it. Disrupting White saviorism removes the power and responsibility from White people and places it squarely in the hands of the leaders of the community it hopes to serve. If you can't serve without power, you're not really serving at all. You're maintaining oppressive power structures and giving yourself a reason to feel good about it.

2. Whiteness Does Not Know Everything

Part of the construct of Whiteness is the idea that White people know best about what communities of color need to heal from the effects of our oppression of them. It's a vicious cycle. Whiteness created a system that made it exponentially more difficult for BIPOC (specifically, Black and Native American populations) to enjoy the same access to resources as White people have. The results of that oppression, among other things, are pervasive social issues such as poverty, hunger, crime, and addiction. Then we look at the people having those experiences and tell them it's their fault that they are poor, hungry, imprisoned, and addicted. Finally, because these people are obviously so incapable of helping themselves, Whiteness decides it needs to swoop in and save the day, and White saviorism is born.

Now, is there personal agency involved here? Yes. Of course there is. But one of the other things Whiteness loves to do is find the "exceptional" Black people who were born poor and made it out through "hard work and perseverance." (Very often, according to the movies at least, they also had a White savior who mentored them into their assimilation.) What Whiteness doesn't like to do, however, is take a good long look at how it perpetuates the systems that keep so many other Black people from succeeding. **Exceptionalism** is a paradigm that Whiteness uses to help it ignore inconvenient truths about its impact in the world by pointing to exceptions to the norm. It also helps Whiteness maintain its assumed superiority (and you know what they say about assumptions).

The Shift

So what's the shift that needs to be made here? A simple three-step process can shift your focus from supremacy to true anti-racism: *relinquish, resource, raze*. First, we need to relinquish our presumption that we know better than BIPOC about what's best for them; BIPOC leadership know what their communities require in order to heal. Second, we recognize that we have access to and can provide the resources they need to embody and practice their own healing. And third, we understand that our work is to raze (dismantle) the systems that perpetuate oppression.

Relinquish. Whiteness needs to understand that we have no idea what sorts of programs will actually work in the communities we have harmed. Rather, we need to relinquish the belief that Whiteness knows best, trust the leaders in those communities to teach us what needs to be done, and submit to their leadership. In most of these communities there are powerful community members *who are already leading* and who have their finger on the pulse of the neighborhood in ways that outsiders never could. They know exactly what the problems are, and they probably have a pretty good idea about how to solve them. Ingenuity doesn't disappear just because someone is poor or marginalized, but it does often go untapped. One of the first ways we can practice anti-racism is to resist the idea that we know better what BIPOC communities need simply because we are White.

Resource. Yes, I'm talking about money here. As I've already pointed out, money is one of the key tools in societies of dominance that keep the oppressed from their rightful liberation. As members of the privileged society, we hold access to resources—specifically money but also other means—that might be missing from the community leadership and keeping them from being as effective as they can be. It may not be as sexy as delivering bagged lunches on your precious Saturday, but some well-planned financial resourcing of BIPOC leaders could be far more effective than a financially sound program led by an uninformed White person or team.

This does speak to the relative pain of resource divestment, and I confess I am being a tiny bit snarky there. By pain, I mean discomfort. Yes, some of your congregation's other programming may need to fall by the wayside, eliciting many complaints and grumbling, but I promise, everyone will survive. I'm here to tell you that true anti-racism really does require you to put your money where your mouth is.

Raze. In *addition* to spending your Saturday afternoon delivering bagged lunches (because again, I'm not saying to ignore hungry bellies), perhaps an organized letter-writing campaign to your elected officials, advocating for policies that combat the causes of systemic poverty or protect our BIPOC siblings from police brutality, for example (while your dollars and other resources are supporting BIPOC leaders), might better serve to develop the institutional change required for the creation of a truly just world. Use your collective bodies to shield protesters at a march. Get political. Organize transportation to the voting booth. Sponsor educational seminars on the issues on the ballot at local, state, and national levels. There are a number of ways you can use your influence as an organization (and teach your congregants how to use their personal agency) to implement change in the world. It's time to understand that our work is to dismantle the systems that perpetuate the problems we want so badly to heal. It's not about passing out Band-Aids. It's about taking away the knife.

3. White churches have much to learn from— and can be served by—BIPOC churches

Here is a paradigm shift that is both nuanced and a little complicated. The idea that White communities can and should be served by BIPOC creates a whole lot of resistance from a whole lot of perspectives. First, it disrupts the idea of White pseudosupremacy. It points to a need within Whiteness that can be filled by BIPOC, which makes Whiteness vulnerable and less powerful. At the same time, there is the very real and very valid truth that the idea of being served by people of color points back to our very problematic (to put it lightly) history with slavery. White communities being served by BIPOC feels uncomfortable in all these ways because it basically takes a really big arrow and points to all of the problems with Whiteness: White hubris, White power, White vulnerability, White history. And if there's one thing we White people love to avoid talking about it's our own Whiteness and its problems.

When I see partnerships between White churches and churches of color, for example, I often sense an unspoken hierarchy. The assumption is that the church of color is the community in need, and the White church is the "savior." Often, this is because the BIPOC church is located in a community with less economic resources than White churches (and this, usually because of racist policies like redlining). Because the White churches control more of the resources, they hold more power, and often wield it in ways that keep the BIPOC churches from truly flourishing and practicing self-determination. But what this economic power also does is fool White churches into thinking that there is nothing that they can learn from BIPOC communities about a whole host of things.

The Shift

The shift here must include a receptivity to being ministered to in deeply spiritual ways combined with a divestment of power—specifically, economic power. That can manifest in a number of ways, but ultimately it means that we relinquish resources and divert them into the hands of BIPOC while also recognizing that we might have spiritual needs that can be met by communities of color. It's often difficult to consider ourselves needy—because it makes it difficult to simultaneously cling to our power.

I also want to acknowledge that even as I write this, I am reinforcing a stereotype of Black poverty, which often also leads in White minds to a false narrative that there is something inherent in Blackness or Brownness that elicits and creates poverty, and that Whiteness is automatically deserving of wealth. We need to resist this narrative by understanding that White people—and yes, even White people who live in middle-class communities and attend wealthy churches—can be experiencing financial difficulties and food insecurity. We need to understand that when the economic standing of BIPOC is entrenched in poverty or struggle it is not because of something inherent in the character but because of something broken in the system. These are important shifts to make in our thinking, because our thinking leads to our behavior.

We can make these shifts by truly partnering (rather than creating a "service dynamic") with the communities with which we wish to enter relationship. For example, we can reach out to local community organizers—those people who are already on the streets doing the work and often know best what the community needs—and ask how we could best support their objectives. We can meet with community leaders (not politicians)—think PTAs, moms' groups, and social service agencies as well as other churches—to discover what the needs are in the community and see if we are uniquely capable of meeting them. In fact, we may even discover that there is mutual need in our congregations that we can work toward in solidarity with these communities. This levels the playing field, because as my colleague Josh has reminded me, as long as your church has something someone else needs, it is in a position of dominance. There are a few important things to remember when we do this, however:

Trust is earned and relationship takes time. Expect to not be taken too seriously, and show up anyway. Especially for predominantly White groups offering support to BIPOC communities, it's incredibly important to understand that they don't owe you their trust. Relationship is an intentional act that takes time and investment, and it's going to take some time before they can trust that you're not there to take over, drop some White saviorism, and then leave.

You don't understand the problem. Even if you think you do, you probably don't. This is why connecting with community organizers is so important. They are the ones standing in the gap, often trying hard to fill a need that the system hasn't even come close to filling. For example, an organization I once worked with that had deep ties to their community and a solid knowledge of what the kids in their neighborhood needed had a grant so that they could use their facility to host at least several dozen at-risk youth from another program, but they only had a van that could fit twelve kids. The grant funds were not allowed to be used for transportation, and so dozens of kids missed out on the opportunity to participate in a program that kept them safe and fed. A White church wanted to come in and guide the organization in how to manage those kids with programming and tutoring and a whole lot of other types of White savioristic advice. But what they really needed was another van or two, and maybe some auto insurance and some drivers. They had the rest covered, thank you very much.

You absolutely, 100 percent, cannot solve the problem. Not by yourself, anyway. Not even with your whole church. You can make a dent. You can be a resource. You can provide extra hands, extra dollars, extra brainpower. But the key here is learning that the real healing power and the real solutions are in the collective, and the collective comes in a whole lot of beautiful colors. It's important to stay in your lane and submit to Black leaders who are solving Black problems, to Indigenous activists who are fighting for Indigenous causes. And when they tell you how Whiteness—and even White saviorism—is doing harm, listen, learn from it, and work to change that behavior. *That's* your lane.

When we think of these partnerships as symbiotic rather than service oriented, we can enjoy a sense of community with others rather than perpetuating a power dynamic. But this is an ethos that needs to be taught to your congregants every step of the way: from the pulpit and at your board meetings, in your volunteer training and the language you use to describe the partnership. Remember from our marketing chapter that everything communicates—so it's important to make sure that everything is communicating what you want it to.

As you consider the ways in which your congregation engages with service projects—both locally and, if it applies, globally—ask yourself these questions and see if you might need to make adjustments. Remember that the adjustments may not happen overnight, but they *do* need to happen.

ASSESSMENT 7.1: MISSIONS AND SERVICE

1. Are you able to define the power dynamics inherent in your service projects? Do they perpetuate White pseudosupremacy or resist it?
2. Define some tangible ways in which you might be able to relinquish control of a service project or ministry and place it in the hands of the community it serves. What scares you about this? What excites you?
3. What are some creative ways that you can resource the communities you serve without controlling them?
4. What activities can your congregation participate in that will help to dismantle systemic racism and its effects?
5. How does your church partner with or support other organizations in the community?
6. If your church is supporting problematic short-mission organizations, what is at stake in ending that support and divesting from this harmful model?
7. What narratives or beliefs inform your church's efforts to serve in poor BIPOC communities? Does this same narrative exist for serving poor White communities?

8

Children and Youth

A man I once knew who was deeply embedded in fundamentalism used to talk a lot about how important it is for churches to help their congregants develop a "proper Christian worldview." The thought always made my spine do a little shudder. *Please do not tinker with my worldview. My worldview and I will figure things out for our own selves, thank you very much.* I think the reason this bothered me so much was because I knew what he really meant, and the worldview he propagated didn't really have a whole lot to do with Jesus, but it did smack of the White cis-hetero-normative patriarchy, with a healthy dose of *A Handmaid's Tale* complementarianism on the side.

Ew.

As I thought more about this tinkering with people's psyches, I realized that while I have no desire to program Christianity into susceptible minds, there is something very enticing about that realm of God into which Jesus invites us. It still feels like something that is not just spiritually nutritious, but something that can manifest in real and beautiful ways here on earth, where our bare feet touch the dirt of this physical space, this place where our spirits are embodied in matter. Far too often, discipleship means initiation into institutions of dominance and inequity, where I am expected to be silent for the sake of unity and to participate in the oppression of my siblings. But when I start to think of what it would actually mean to disciple the world into the ways of Jesus—not to convert souls into some false sense of "rightness" and membership into some sort of exclusive religious club, but rather into a new way to love the world and its people—then I start to get excited.

I confess I approached writing this chapter with a sense of fear and dread, not because I think children and youth are unimportant or unworthy of my time and effort, but because they are, perhaps, the *most important* part of this work. On the path to racial justice, there are two tracks of becoming: the BIPOC track, where the work is that of self-love and self-actualization, healing from both micro and macro racial trauma, and thriving in a world that offers more obstacles than opportunity; and the track for White people, which is about resisting the construct of Whiteness, both within our own psyches and out there in the world, while learning to love ourselves even as we embody privilege. Assuming that most people reading this book are over the age of seven, this means that we have our work cut out for us, because by the time you put this book into your Amazon cart, our personalities were already pretty well formed. But when we think about the environment we offer to our children and youth—and when we think about how we invite them to cocreate the realm of God as Jesus would—well. Things start to get exciting, because we are standing in the deep pool of potential. That's exciting work.

It's also slightly terrifying in the weight of its responsibility. Hence, my fear and dread.

In this chapter, I want us to explore the ways that we can resist the racial construction that is fighting for space in the forming psyches of our young people, and to do so intentionally. I want us to realize that our Sunday school classrooms and our youth groups can be responsible for forming either the next generation of "good White racists"[1] or a world that more closely resembles the beloved community, the banquet table of Jesus and the realm of God. I want to help us all understand our Sunday school classrooms as not just another ministry or line item on the budget, but as a deeply important, formative movement for a more just and equitable future. (But hey—no pressure.)

In order to do this, we'll explore the larger ideas of identity formation and acculturation, as well as the different roles BIPOC and White people play in a world imbued with White pseudosupremacy. Throughout the chapter, we'll also discuss strategies that you can apply in your children's and youth ministries that can help you disciple your young people into a worldview centered on *justice*. It is of course important to audit the books, toys, and curricula we use in our children's and youth ministry, but we *also* need to understand and intentionally teach anti-racist dynamics to our children. We *can* raise up a generation of children who are racially aware and conscious, who will hopefully in turn create a world in which racism is just as uncool as being the schoolyard bully is today.

IDENTITY FORMATION AND RACE

One of the ways that pseudosupremacy maintains itself is by remaining invisible, especially to White people, and one of the most convenient places for this to happen is through the normative practices that take place in classrooms. Combine the power and authority of the classroom with the supreme and ultimate authority and power of God, and let's just say your Sunday school classroom and youth group programs can quickly become places that either sow deep self-worth and self-love, or that disfigure White souls, foster internalized racism in BIPOC, and perpetuate our pseudosupremacist culture.

In order to understand how this works, we need to understand **acculturation,** the process by which BIPOC assume the standards of the dominant White culture. It is also a process of racial trauma, because even for BIPOC who are born in the United States, the process of accommodating themselves to White culture begins at birth.[2] It is important to understand, however, that acculturation into Whiteness doesn't happen just for BIPOC. White-bodied people also experience a process by which they are ascribed Whiteness and learn to live by its rules and norms.

Tools of acculturation include things like the stories we tell and who the heroes are in those stories. It's important to remember that diversity is not the only marker for an anti-racist book, because a story can have a diverse cast of characters, but if the BIPOC characters are disempowered or represented in negative ways, it reinforces White norms as ideal. This can happen in subtle ways. For example, a story about a young boy whose primary language is Spanish can highlight the struggles he encounters in a predominantly English-speaking school, but it can do it in a way that devalues his language of origin by making it seem less desirable than English, or it can celebrate his tenacity and ability to master more than one language while also honoring his culture and language of origin. These are subtle differences that create situations of acculturation.

What is key to understand is that the process of acculturation into Whiteness (for both BIPOC and White people) requires self-betrayal.

For example, White children might resist a desire to be friends with Black children because somewhere they received the message that they should "stay with their own kind," and the pressure to maintain ties with their known social group is strong. Or they might resist their inherent sense of fairness and stay silent when they see BIPOC children being disciplined more harshly, for fear of drawing attention to themselves and their own Whiteness. BIPOC, meanwhile, having learned about the values of White culture, practice being **racially innocuous,** a self-defensive, self-protective habit of behaving "in ways that may soften their racial, ethnic, and cultural expression so as not to stand out." This means that for BIPOC, navigating White spaces might include changing how they speak (**code switching**), dress, or eat when they are in spaces such as predominantly White stores and schools.[3]

All of these point to the maintenance of White culture as the norm. **White culture** can be described as the set of Western beliefs and values that prioritize "rugged individualism, competition, action-orientation, hierarchical power structures, standard American English, linear and future time orientation, Judeo-Christianity, European history, Protestant work ethic, objective science, owning goods and property, the nuclear family unit, and European aesthetics."[4] The point here is that White culture perpetuates itself by maintaining itself as the "normal and healthy" way to be, and because it is normalized, it is invisible to White people—kids and adults alike—while it disfigures our souls by making us resistant to, intolerant of, and terrified of racial difference. Meanwhile, BIPOC children are given the message that they will eternally and perpetually never quite measure up—that there is something inherently wrong about their very being, a perpetual miswire in their existence. In both cases, this is a horrific and heartbreaking wound that we can and must resist and heal. And we can start in our Sunday school classrooms and our youth groups by offering different narratives that first and foremost render all of this visible to everyone as early as we start to play. Because we can't resist that which we do not see.

Let me state here clearly and forcefully a very important point, because if you're like me, your Whiteness might be coming out to play here, trying to convince you that children of such a tender age don't need to tackle such difficult topics as racism. You might even convince yourself that the Black kids you care about might escape it so long as you don't mention it. Let me assure you that it's not a matter of if but when BIPOC kids have their first racialized experience, and if they have to survive the experience, then White kids sure as hell can manage to muster up the strength to learn about it. In fact, your White kids might surprise you with how well they can break this stuff down for you. If you're like me, you might just find yourself schooled by your preschooler. But if you avoid the topic because you think your White children are somehow too frail to face the reality of their Whiteness? Well, you're just twisting the knife a little deeper into their White, disfigured little souls. You are also complicit, because you're letting them grow into adults who are too frail to confront their own Whiteness later on, when they have the power to influence change.

UNDERSTANDING RACIAL IDENTITY DEVELOPMENT

(Bryana)

Understanding racial identity development increases our ability to act more consciously as racial beings. I did not learn about racial identity development until my thirties. It was one of the most transformational and liberating experiences for me. I was finally able to name and to better understand the lived experiences of my childhood, adolescence, and adulthood. As I have unpacked each stage of my racial identity, I have come to realize how critical it is for us to equip our own children, both our biological children and those in our sphere of influence, with an understanding of their own racial identity development.

I have facilitated race equity workshops for a lot of predominantly White groups, and it never seems to fail that someone will eventually bring up a "hopeful" message that sounds something like this: "Our children don't see color; they don't tolerate the kinds of things that were tolerated when I was growing up." A personal plea: please do not fool yourself into believing this myth. Educate yourself, so that you can be a teacher for our children. Racism is not going away in the next generation. Justice doesn't stand a chance if we do not name the harmful impact of individual, systemic, and **color-blind racism.** In order to do that, we must understand the myth of race (which includes a lot of unlearning: unlearning of harmful ideologies, partial truths, and untruths that we have been indoctrinated into since our childhood) and be willing to embrace the hard truths we uncover.

Embracing the hard truth that race is a myth, yet it has significant impact in our society today, looks like a radical love that allows us to naturally find value and beauty in all races and ethnicities. It also looks like radical acceptance of our shared humanity, where we embrace each other's full identities.

My journey to racial awakening was not linear. As my consciousness around my racial identity has been fluid, so has my desire to self-identify differently, because racial identity has a different layer of complexity for multiracial people. It wasn't until my thirties when I felt pride in my Blackness, and when I first had an innate drive to take back my power as a Black woman.

Racial identity is often imposed upon BIPOC folks, but our power can also be reclaimed through our racial identity. For example, I have self-identified as no racial identity, mixed race, biracial, Black, and currently as a biracial Black woman. As I write this, I am reconsidering naming my racial identity as Afro-American. As I continue to unpack my indoctrination into Whiteness, I am reminded of many experiences that shaped my racial identity. I will share three in particular to validate how critical racial identity formation is, and how early it starts in children. Our children, from the moment they come into this world, are never immune from race and racial identity. They receive verbal and visual messages about their own race and the race of others through the media, in cartoons, in books, at church, at the grocery store, in the doctor's office, in school—everywhere.

Hair. As a young biracial girl, I subconsciously found ways to assimilate into the dominant White spaces I was in. Beautiful meant straight, flowing hair. As a young girl, I hated going to pool parties because I would often be the only BIPOC child there, and after a fun afternoon in the water, I would come out of the pool with my hair looking like I had been electrocuted. My hair would tighten and frizz up as it dried, while all of my friends' hair would look nowhere near as unruly as mine did. From an early age, I noticed that strangers, family, and friends alike would shower me with compliments any time I wore my hair straight. This subtle but powerful **anti-Blackness** is embedded in the psyche of most people born or raised in America. Even my Black family would encourage chemical and heat straightening, because I "had that good hair." That essentially meant that my hair would respond well to chemical and heat straightening. It was my Black family who introduced me and my mother to straightening products at the beauty supply store.

I would beg my mom to chemically relax my hair every six to eight weeks so it would be "straight." The longer I left the straightening chemical on my hair, the straighter it would become—and the more

RACIAL IDENTITY AND AFROS

Black women's identity and their relationship with their hairstyle are intrinsically linked. One cannot exist without the other. When it comes to hair, most men and women can relate. Most people of all races agonize over how to style it, and in some cases how not to lose it. But not all hair is created equal:

> For centuries, from the continent of Africa to America, Black hair has been a symbol of cultural identity, spirituality, character, and beauty. In the 17th century, when Europeans began stealing men, women and children from their homeland in mass numbers, they sought ways to further dehumanize them by shaving off their hair. It was a symbolic removal of African culture. To further dehumanize them, Europeans used unfavorable, demeaning descriptions in reference to African hair. Enslaved men and women either had to shave their heads or cover their hair. This evolved into African beauty being racialized, and European looks and hairstyles being the accepted image of beauty.[5]

This is the fundamental reason why it is wildly inappropriate to ask a BIPOC if you can touch their hair. And I would go even further by saying it is inappropriate to call out a BIPOC hairstyle in a way that implies it is exotic or unusual (even if that is "hidden" within a compliment). If White people are in awe about Black hair, it is likely because it is foreign to them, which means they have lived a life of segregation, and that truth has barely been a blip on their radar. Their shock-and-awe reaction regarding a Black person's hair further perpetuates the age-old exoticizing of Black men and women. It also objectifies them. It "others" them. Our children are internalizing messages regarding their physical appearance from a very early age, and even with good intentions, we run the risk of giving BIPOC children a racial identity complex.

There is an underlying message for people of color in a White-dominated society: Blend in. Be like us. Look like us. Act like us. I internalized messages I was hearing in the media and in my networks that distinguished certain Black hairstyles as more professional than others. I would spend hours on the weekends washing and heat-straightening my hair for the workweek. On rainy or humid days, I spent hours worrying about how the weather would affect my hair. I would choose not to go to the pool on the weekends because that meant more work to do to prep my hair for the workweek. Adia Harvey Wingfield describes the plight of people of color in the workplace:

> Minority professionals tread cautiously to avoid upsetting the majority group's sensibilities. Put simply, they can be visibly black, but don't want to be perceived as stereotypically black. . . . A black female candidate for a law firm who chemically straightens her hair, is in a nuclear family structure, and resides in a predominantly white neighborhood signals a fealty to (often unspoken) racial norms. She does so in a way that an equally qualified black woman candidate who wears dreadlocks, has a history of pushing for racial change in the legal field, is a single mother, and lives in the inner city does not.[6]

scalp burns I would get. But they quickly scabbed and went away. It was worth it, to fit in. As I reflect back on this, I am heartbroken for my younger self, and for all the young Black and multiracial girls with beautiful and kinky hair who believe the path to beauty is to literally harm their own bodies (with scalp burns) to assimilate into Whiteness.

In middle school, I went to a hair salon with a White friend and her mother. I remember the hairstylist looking at my hair with a confused look on her face, almost as if her inner voice was saying: "What the hell am I supposed to do with this Black girl's hair?!?" The salon was clearly for White people, but somehow, I found myself sitting in the chair, scalp burning, with a chemical relaxer on my hair. The White hairstylist left it on far too long, but I didn't say anything. I didn't want to call even more attention to my Blackness. About a week after that appointment, my hair started falling out. I ended up with a bald spot on the top of my head. My friend's mother completely dismissed my mom when she made mention of it, as if it was my fault for having "weird" hair. This attachment I had to straight hair continued into my adulthood and into the workplace. I spent thousands of dollars to continue suppressing my natural hair texture.

As I have matured in my understanding and embraced my racial identity—despite the dominant cultural norms—one of the physical ways I have expressed this "coming home" is by "going natural"—I stopped chemically relaxing my hair and now wear it in all its natural glory. I consider this decision to reflect my emergence out of Whiteness and immersion into the Black community. I find myself in this stage quite often, as I have a great desire to connect with Black folks as a way to validate who I am and my experiences connected with my Blackness.

On my own for the first time. Right out of college, I started working for a White-male-dominated company in a White-male-dominated industry. My first sales territory was in Texas, and prior to moving, I received "the talk" from my father about the specific towns that I was to avoid—not even a stop for gas—because they were not safe for BIPOC. This was the first time I had "the talk" with my dad regarding what towns I was to avoid because, unknown to me at the time, the KKK was still very active in many parts of the United States.[7] (KKK groups are largely concentrated in the southern and eastern parts of the nation, and Texas currently has at least fifty-four different hate groups, according to the Southern Poverty Law Center.[8]) While I was mostly excited about this new adventure, moving far from the safety of my home for the first time as a young woman was already somewhat scary, and my race further compounded that anxiety.

When I was a child, race was never a topic of conversation in my family. As a thirty-something-year-old, I am just now having more intimate conversations with my Black father to better understand *why* it wasn't something we talked about. As I continue to dig deep, I'm recognizing the innate desire in my dad to keep us safe. I'm also understanding his own need, personally, to assimilate (as much as he could as a Black man) to survive and "thrive." I've also wondered why there was such avid support (and encouragement) for me to straighten my hair rather than embrace its beauty. My mother is White, so she had no idea how to manage Black hair, and she, at the time, was willing to do whatever would help me to feel beautiful. Even if that meant straightening my hair.

I went to a very segregated school, worshiped in an all-White church, lived in a predominantly White neighborhood. Nothing equipped me to manage racism and my own racial identity as a child. Second to school, I spent most of my time at church or at church functions. Imagine if the church my family attended had been better equipped to shape not only their children's racial identity and race consciousness, but also to influence our parents' ability to raise race-conscious children. I do know one thing: it would have been life-changing for me and my family.

Church as an adult. About five years ago, my husband and I moved to Raleigh, North Carolina, from Indianapolis. We immediately found a church home at a United Methodist church right around the corner from where we lived. I was raised in the UMC, and while I had attended church quite a bit since moving away from home after college, I had not found a church I considered "home." Our North Carolina church pews were predominantly filled with White folks, but it felt like home because that was what I was used to. While I was bothered by the lack of racial diversity, I did not see it as any different from any other church I had attended. Sundays, after all, are the most segregated days of the week. It was not until I started getting involved with a local African Methodist Episcopal church that I started to experience unraveling.

Our pastor had built a relationship with the AME pastor after reaching out to him following the murder of nine worshipers at Mother Emanuel AME Church in Charleston, South Carolina. We started a book study with this church, reading Jim Wallis's book *America's Original Sin*. I began forming a relationship with members of this church, and my pastor asked me to help him continue investing in this relationship and connecting the churches, because he did not have a lot of time and didn't want the relationship to fizzle out. At the time, I was excited. I was not initially bothered by it.

As I got deeper and deeper into this faith community, I started experiencing moments that caused me frustration and anger, but at the time I could not name why. I jumped into planning community events for neighboring churches to learn about systemic racism and discuss the role of the church in dismantling racism. My pastor never showed up. Very few people from my church showed up. I would plan potlucks with the local AME church for people to gather and be in a relationship together. I started noticing I was the only one initiating these events. I wanted to see action outside of our church, with local grassroots organizations, and that required funding. Unfortunately, in a wealthy church there was not a dollar to be found to invest in racial equity work.

This predominantly White faith community was part of a parish model, with three other campuses operating as individual churches yet tied to a "family covenant." Three of the campuses were predominantly White, and one campus was Hispanic/Latinx. I eventually connected with the Hispanic/Latinx faith campus. We started engaging in race equity work together, and I became even more connected and aware of the hurdles that this Latinx campus had experienced for the past twelve years. On one hand, the (White) church leaders would express how important it is to them to be a community who cares about all of God's children, while at the same time, they "could not" preach it from the pulpit and they "could not" invest financially in this work. But simultaneously, they were proud to be a multicultural church and tokenize their Latinx faith community as well as the only Black woman (me) in one of their White campuses.

During our last season as regular Sunday worshipers at this church, I was pregnant with our first son. I started noticing more clearly how White the children's programs were. And that the youth of the church were not at all in close proximity to the racial justice work (mostly performative as it was) that was happening. I finally made the decision that I could not do the work of racial justice and equity in the same community that I was attending for my spiritual growth and development. I also couldn't imagine raising my son in a church that wasn't able to name the harm of racism and the role it played in it, and to teach the truth about Jesus as undoubtedly the most political, justice-oriented person of his time.

We left the church. We left the first family we met when we moved here. While we still maintain friendships there at a surface level, I still harbor feelings of frustration and anger. I am exhausted by their performance allyship and their inability to see the harm they are causing to people they claim to love. My experience as a young girl (and, eventually, woman) in a predominantly White church shaped my church experience as an adult biracial Black woman. My lived experience further inspires me to be more conscious of the ways in which race and racism in the church shape our children in profound ways. My husband and I left this church because we wanted a different experience for our son. It is critical as a church leader to recognize the importance of resisting the normalization of White culture in the church, starting with our children.

MICRO- AND MACROAGGRESSIONS, INTERVENTIONS, AND ALLYSHIP

A church that wants to be anti-racist will therefore begin its work of resistance in its children's programming, understanding that the foundations of racism and supremacy culture are laid in childhood. A part of that work is about intentionally understanding—and teaching— what it means to be an ally, how to recognize micro- and macroaggressions as they happen, and how to intervene when they do.

But first, I need to acknowledge that the anti-racism lexicon is quickly changing. By the time you figure out how to be an ally, "allyship," as an anti-racism term, is coming under fire, and you've barely just gotten started. It's good news that the vocabulary is changing because it means progress is happening, but it can also be confusing. We need to remember first and foremost not to cling too tightly to the words we use because we do not yet have language that describes a world in which supremacy culture does not exist. As we struggle to find one, we may also stumble over words, and phrases may come and go quickly. Let's let go of the words and talk about the ideas. Hopefully the words will suffice.

In this case, I want to talk about the difference between being an **ally,** an **accomplice,** and a **coconspirator.** Educator and activist Brittany Packnett explained it best when she said that "an ally shows up when it's convenient. An accomplice shows up when there's a risk. A coconspirator goes into the risk proactively, because they understand that they helped create the pain in the first place."[9] Our job is not just to help White kids develop into effective coconspirators, but ultimately to create a world in which the need for coconspirators no longer exists. Until that happens, however, we can help our children understand racialized dynamics and the roles people play within them: targets, allies (we'll stick with this term for now), and bystanders.

Targets are members of marginalized communities (BIPOC, LGBTQ+, women) who experience micro- and macroaggressions regularly and who need to develop strategies for self-protection and self-care. Allies (coconspirators) are those members of the dominant group (White people, men, heterosexuals) who seek to actively work to eradicate prejudicial practices they witness in their personal or professional lives. Bystanders are those who witness or become aware of unjust situations that are worthy of comment or action.[10] These identities are fluid at any given time, and often overlap, but there's an important difference between bystanders and allies (coconspirators): "Most bystanders experience themselves as good, moral and decent human beings who move about in an invisible veil of Whiteness, [and] have minimal awareness of themselves as a racial/cultural being." Allies, on the other hand, "are more likely to have an evolved awareness of themselves as racial/cultural beings, and to be more attuned to sociopolitical dynamics of race and racism."[11]

In a world in which White pseudosupremacy reigns, microaggressions are, in some ways, the front lines of interpersonal anti-racism work. If we want to create an anti-racist future, teaching children about microaggressions should be a part of their education in basic manners and etiquette. After all, if children are capable of learning to say *please* and *thank you*, they are also able to understand that it's not cool to touch a Black person's hair just because they want to. Microaggressions are literally exhausting for BIPOC and are often a source of personal conflict for would-be coconspirators. A **microaggression** is defined as

> the everyday, subtle, intentional—and oftentimes unintentional— interactions or behaviors that communicate some sort of bias toward historically marginalized groups. The difference between microaggressions and overt discrimination or macroaggressions, is that people who commit microaggressions might not even be aware of them.[12]

Common examples of microaggressions include touching Black hair or making comments like "She's Black, but she's really smart" or "You're so articulate." Asking a person of Asian descent where they're "really" from—even when it is obvious that they are American—is also common, as is explaining to BIPOC how you're totally not racist because of your Black coworker, who you assume is your friend. (You might be surprised to discover he considers you a colleague, and that he holds a higher bar than working together for friendship.)

Macroaggressions, on the other hand, happen on a grander scale against whole people groups; the insistence by certain political players (some now unelected, I'm happy to say) to call the coronavirus that caused the global pandemic of 2020 the "Chinese Virus" is an excellent example of a macroaggression. Neither micro- nor macroaggressions happen in vacuum. They occur most often surrounded by White embodiment, and that White embodiment can either represent White pseudosupremacy or it can represent anti-racism. As churches who care about this work, who wish to exist as radically anti-racist, we have a responsibility to do our part to usher in the realm of God here on earth, and there's no way we can do that without intentionally working to raise up a beautiful generation of coconspirators for justice.

Start now.

THE COCONSPIRATOR CLASSROOM

Now that we are beginning to understand the racial dynamics of acculturation, microaggressions, and allyship, it's time to dive into the nuts and bolts of what this looks like in the classroom. When it comes to developing coconspirators in our children's and youth ministries, there are a few goals:

1. Help all children to develop a healthy awareness of racial identity—their own, and that of others. Whole books can be written on this topic, and I am not an expert in child development or education, so please understand that this is a surface-level treatment at best, but it's an important piece of spiritual formation. The first thing that is imperative in developing healthy racial identities in both BIPOC and White children is to render the invisible visible. In other words, in churches that are predominantly White, we must resist Whiteness as the standardizing norm and speak about it not as a monolith but as one of many. This will do the work of both resisting pseudosupremacy in White children and reinforcing a healthy sense of self-worth in BIPOC.

2. Help all children develop a deep sense of holistic self-love and self-worth, especially through a racial lens. One of the biggest obstacles to developing a healthy White identity is **White guilt**. One of the key reasons White people tend to resist anti-racism is a desire to avoid this negative feeling, and that's understandable. No one wants to feel guilty for being born into a skin color they didn't choose. (Sounds familiar, right?) For White kids to learn a sense of White self-love and self-worth, we need to move them from the useless feeling of White guilt toward the idea of White responsibility. They can learn that White-bodied people who experience privilege have the responsibility to resist racism, privilege, microaggressions, and pseudosupremacy when they see them happening—and we need to teach them how to see it happening by resisting Whiteness as the standardizing norm. Kids know when something's not right—but they may not have the language to describe what they know. As anti-racist adults working to teach them, giving them the language and helping them understand how to have conversations about race early in life is an important aspect of anti-racism and a healthy sense of racial self-love.

For BIPOC kids, representation matters. In order to resist Whiteness as the standardizing norm, BIPOC kids need to see themselves in the stories you tell, the books you read, the toys they play with, the pictures on the wall. This is healthy and good for White kids, too. Seeing themselves represented in positive stereotypes rather than negative ones, in leadership roles, in everyday occurrences represented in the media and curriculum you provide, will all go a long way toward developing healthy racial identities in BIPOC children and helping them resist internalized racism.

3. Prepare BIPOC children to be resilient and well equipped to recognize and handle microaggressions when they occur. Self-love and self-worth are important aspects of resilience in BIPOC children, because when a strong and healthy racial self-identity is embedded in their psyches and they are presented with a racist event, they will be more likely to assume the problem is outside of them—in other words, they'll think the other guy's a jerk, not that there is something wrong with them. Of course, racist incidents are always harmful and horrifically difficult, and so children also need to be given ample opportunity to discuss these events and their feelings about them. Providing examples of how other children have successfully managed when they have been targeted is not just a great way to equip BIPOC children for when this happens to them, but it's also a great way for White children to build understanding and empathy for the BIPOC experience, making them much more likely to be active coconspirators for justice. And it's a perpetuating cycle, because the more BIPOC are surrounded by White people who are anti-racist, the more they'll receive confirmation that the problem is not them, but rather the person exhibiting racism. If we work to build a generation of anti-racists, we can literally render racism uncool, and racists will be the outliers.

4. Prepare White children to be well-resourced coconspirators who are able to recognize and intervene during racially unjust circumstances. The first thing my kids learned when they stepped onto the mats at martial arts school is, when confronted by a bully, to put their hands up, palms open and facing out, and to say in a loud voice, "Stop messing with me!" The technique is multifaceted. It places them in a posture that is ready for self-defense—hands up and open, ready to grab a collar or ball into a fist if absolutely necessary—but it's also nonthreatening. The command to stop messing with them is loud and assertive, giving their aggressor pause—maybe this kid is not the pushover they thought they were. But it's also more than that. By saying in a loud voice, "Stop messing with me!" they are drawing the attention of all the people around them, and with that one statement and their body posture, they are clearly displaying what is going on here: they are not the aggressor, they are being attacked. Their words say they are being messed with; their open palms convey that they are not in fighting mode but in a protective stance. Everyone who sees them will understand in a moment what's happening and ideally will intervene.

These kids are well equipped for the scenario taking place. If kids can be prepared to manage potential violence in this way, we can also equip White kids to manage racist contexts and microaggressions when they occur.

It often comes down to two things: first, kids need to understand when a racist event is occurring; second, they need to know what to say when it does. Offering examples of microaggressions and appropriate responses to them is paramount. (While we are of course talking about race here, we should note that microaggressions happen to girls and LGBTQ+ kids as well, and we can train our kids to address these too.) Teaching kids how to make these behaviors uncool by demonstrating solidarity with the child who is being targeted can be incorporated into any antibullying curriculum but needs to be contextualized for racism. And paying attention to how this is important in the realm of God especially shouldn't be that hard to do, if the God we worship is the anti-racist I'm pretty sure God is.

We can teach our children and youth to clearly state that racist jokes aren't cool, and that no, it's never OK to touch another person's body without their consent—not even their hair. We can teach them to use disapproving body language and to demonstrate shock and dismay when a friend uses racist language. We can instruct them to place their bodies next to those being targeted to demonstrate solidarity.

Perhaps even more important, however, is to teach White children how to accept correction when they make a racial mistake, because most likely, they will make a racial mistake. It might be innocent curiosity, it might be embedded racism, it might be a misunderstanding, or it might be totally on purpose—but when a White kid acts like a racist jerk, we need to teach our kids how to receive that criticism, make reparations, and be reinstated back into community. Learning how to take responsibility for our actions, our words, and the harm we do is part of what it means to grow up, and it is a key tool in dismantling White pseudosupremacy culture, White guilt, and racism.

A NOTE ON CURRICULUM

Children's and youth curricula that are imbued with Whiteness abound, and now that you have more awareness about racial identity formation in both White and BIPOC children, it's time to do the hard work of auditing our current materials and ensuring that they do not reinforce supremacy culture. This will take an eye for the subtle as well as the overt, and if possible, your lesson plans should be reviewed by BIPOC. If that's not possible, however, you'll have to do the work to see what you may not normally see. Does the material appropriate non-White cultures to teach a lesson? Does it render some cultures less valuable, civilized, or worthy of others? How does it perpetuate White standards and values as ideal (for example, individualism over the collective, perfectionism and the Protestant work ethic over rest and relationship)?

As you review your teaching materials, you'll want to be sure not only that racist or pseudosupremacist propaganda is missing, but also that anti-racist information is present. Kids (and probably many adults) need to be equipped with an anti-racist tool kit, because although none of us is born a racist per se, the indoctrination is swift and effective. Therefore, it takes an intentional intervention early to resist it.

One of the best ways to raise White kids who are actively anti-racist is to make sure they are comfortable talking about race, because color-blind racism is one of the most effective ways that subtle supremacy exerts itself. It renders BIPOC identities not invisible to White people—because we all know we see it—but unimportant (until it becomes an issue for White people). If it is unimportant, it becomes far easier to not see racism when it happens, to say things like "All Lives Matter," or to deny that race might be involved in issues such as police brutality. The sooner White children learn that racial identity is real and how to talk about it, the sooner we'll be able to create the anti-racist society we all hope for.

ASSESSMENT 8.1: CHILDREN AND YOUTH

Curriculum Review

1. Review the materials you teach in your class. Do they reinforce supremacy culture? If so, how?
2. Is there adequate racial representation across your materials? If not, how can this be corrected?
3. How do your materials render Whiteness invisible and normalizing? How can you resist this?
4. Does your curriculum center BIPOC voices and represent Jesus as concerned about justice in the Bible stories you highlight?

5. Does your curriculum give your students a viewpoint of the Bible from those in the margins?
6. Does your curriculum relegate non-White cultures as less than, or somehow devalue them?

Classroom Review

1. Are the toys and books available in the classroom racially representative?
2. Do the images that hang on the walls represent varied racial identities in positive ways?
3. How is God represented to your children? Is God a White man? Are there other ways to represent God to your children that are more representative of God's creation?

9

Pastoral Care

I want to begin this chapter by telling you that if you perform pastoral care in any capacity, you are officially a badass, and I bow to you. I went to seminary not because I wanted to be a pastor, but more because I am a truth teller and I wanted to know the specific theological arguments for what I knew in my heart to be true. But I know enough about myself to understand that I would probably not be the most . . . *pastoral* pastor. But you—*you* are the heroic ones who offer people the holy and sacred gift of your presence during the most painful parts of their lives. You are the heroes who run into the emotional and spiritual equivalents of burning buildings and car wrecks, and that is some kind of superpower I simply don't have. My deep regards.

So now that we've established that you are basically a superhero with a collar instead of a cape, let's dig in to how to be *anti-racist* superheroes. I have become convinced that anti-racism work in the church is a matter of urgent pastoral care, and treating the wound of Whiteness is paramount. We need to understand that our liberation is collective, woven together into the same tapestry of harm and potential. Very often, when we think about anti-racism work, our minds jump to how we can better care for and offer healing to our Black and Brown siblings, and this is absolutely imperative and needs to be a priority. Sometimes, that might mean taking action, and sometimes it might mean stepping back into our own lane. But the part that White people often miss is that *anti-racism work requires White healing*. When we truly understand this, and when we recognize that true anti-racism must include—and indeed is rooted in—White inner work that translates into real action toward dismantling racist systems, we will begin to treat this wound rather than ignoring it and letting it fester. If we wish to care for souls, this is a part of holistic care that I believe has been missing for quite some time. It's time to get started.

In order to talk about this, we have to be willing to acknowledge both collective and individual racial trauma. As a White person offering pastoral care, you may find yourself in a helping position with a member of the BIPOC community or a fellow White person, and the thing I want to make clear is that *both of them carry racial trauma in their bodies and their psyches.* Worse, it's a baseline trauma that undergirds the acute crisis for which they may be seeking counsel. In other words, racial trauma is a constant current running through the lives of your congregants and is something they have to deal with every day. BIPOC and LGBTQ+ communities may be more acutely aware of the traumas they encounter as marginalized members of society, but when it comes to their own *racial* trauma, White people are probably completely clueless as to how racial trauma operates in their lives.

Before I continue this conversation, I need to make two important points. First, the racial trauma that White people experience is very different from that which BIPOC experience; I am not making an argument of equivalency here, and I am most definitely not calling the discomfort the average White person feels when confronted with their own racism "trauma." White people experience something called perpetrator trauma, which I'll define shortly. I am saying that the White soul is wounded, and in order for justice to prevail, this White wound needs to heal. Second, I want to expand our understanding of trauma beyond the concept of a single, catastrophic event that changes our lives forever to include small, everyday experiences that require hypervigilance and create the perception of a loss of control. We'll talk about that in a bit, too.

I am not saying that when the next person crosses your office door in crisis due to the death of a spouse or an addicted child, you should start spouting off anti-racist rhetoric because that's what a good anti-racist pastor would do. No—but what I am saying is that we cannot treat and support only parts of an individual; we must treat the whole. In order to do that, we must be willing and able to recognize the racialized contexts in which they move and live, and how that may be impacting their situation—even if they don't see them for themselves.

PERPETRATOR TRAUMA AND MORAL VICTIMHOOD

In order to understand the concept of perpetrator trauma, we first need a working definition of trauma itself. As a psychological condition, **trauma** can be defined as "a response to an experience that renders an individual unable to properly process that experience," which can result in symptoms that include "flashbacks, nightmares, feelings of alienation, diminished empathy, or avoidance of reminders of the initial trauma."[1] In a fascinating article on perpetrator trauma and mass atrocity, Saira Mohamed claims that because of the sympathy we feel for victims of violence, the concept of trauma "has shifted from a neutral category that identifies an experience that is universal . . . to a label that validates, even extols, the suffering of those whose experiences warrant recognition." She goes on to say, "Trauma is not merely a psychological disorder; it is a moral category that identifies its subject as a person who merits empathy and deserves to be heard."[2] In other words, we tend to believe that only victims experience trauma, because to wear the badge of trauma is some sort of moral signifier of validity.

Perpetrators of violence, on the other hand, are dehumanized by our desire to distance ourselves from them—perpetrators must be monsters of some sort; they can't possibly be human like the rest of us—and so perpetrators are denied the full human experience of also experiencing trauma, especially trauma induced by their own acts of violence. But shifting trauma back into a neutral category can give us valuable insight not just into how trauma works, but also how regular human beings come to do very bad things. Our first paradigm shift, then, is to understand **perpetrator trauma** as the neutral psychological response of perpetrators to their own violent actions that displays all the symptoms of victim trauma, even as they are not victims themselves.

EVERYDAY TRAUMA AND BETRAYAL OF SELF

In her book *How to Do the Work,* Nicole LePera redefines trauma, which she claims the majority of mental health practitioners understand to be the result of a catastrophic event, meaning that only people who experience something acute, singular, and powerful can experience trauma. She believes, however, "that our understanding of trauma should be widened to include a diverse range of overwhelming experiences or, as the neurologist Robert Scaer defined it, any negative life event 'that occurs in a state of relative helplessness."[3] Though the traditional psychological tools for gauging trauma are useful, LePera claims they don't tell the full story, and that they do not "take into account the range of emotional and spiritual traumas, which are an outgrowth of consistently denying or repressing the needs of the authentic Self that many of us have experienced."[4]

LePera makes it clear throughout her book that traumatic experiences aren't always obvious and that trauma has more to do with our response to our experiences than to the events themselves. Very often, trauma is the result of self-betrayal and feelings of helplessness or lack of choice. We are traumatized when we lack a sense of control, voice, or power, or when we feel we must self-betray in order to gain the love, affection, or attention of our primary caregivers:

> Trauma occurred when we consistently betrayed ourselves for love, were consistently treated in a way that made us feel unworthy or unacceptable resulting in a severed connection to our authentic Self. Trauma creates the fundamental belief that we must betray who we are in order to survive.[5]

In other words, a person can experience trauma from seemingly normal occurrences that happen every day, especially if those situations cause that person to consistently betray their own needs and desires in order to get the love and the care that they need to live. We learn these behaviors in our earliest years, and it takes awareness, hard work, and willpower to practice agency over them as adults.

WHITE TRAUMA

At the core of racist ideology is a set of basic human emotions that drive our desire to cling to our Whiteness: fear, guilt/shame, and isolation. These emotions feed off each other and work below the White consciousness to perpetuate racism even in those who wish to banish it. That's why, in matters of pastoral care, it's imperative to understand the ways in which these existential pressures—which exist on both the individual and the societal levels—are in operation at any given time.

At the root of our pseudosupremacy is one of the most basic human emotions: fear. Born out of a need for survival, fear serves the human brain well by initiating our self-protective instincts, recognizing and categorizing danger, and motivating us to find our in-group—the people who are like us—and find ways to dehumanize those who are not like us, the Other. White people have been born into and raised in a culture that regularly others BIPOC as radically different from us, and we have witnessed over and over again the horrific treatment of Black and Brown bodies by White violence. We remain safe as long as we manage to hold on to power; as long as we are in power, we stave off the retribution that we believe would happen if we lost it.

Which brings us to the guilt/shame dynamic. White fear is generated by the feelings of guilt and shame that we suppress every day and try to pretend aren't there. It's important to understand the difference between guilt and shame, and the easiest way to break it down is to say that guilt is based on external behavior, while shame is carried internally and refers first and foremost to the self. Within the White racial context, guilt therefore relates to our association with the atrocities perpetrated by our skin kin. Shame, on the other hand, is an inside job. Less about the collective, this is about a splitting off from one's self.

In her book *Learning to Be White,* Thandeka offers an excellent exploration of White shame, which she claims occurs when White children are required to self-betray (severing a friendship with a Black friend, for example) in order to maintain their connections with their caregivers and family of origin as a matter of survival.[6] The result is a fracturing of self as the White child either denies their desire for relationship with the Black child or denies their need for caregiving. Here is the traumatizing self-betrayal LePera speaks about. For a young child unable to care for themselves, the choice is obvious, but they experience a deep shame for wanting something—relationship with the other child—that is, for some reason they can't understand, arbitrarily "wrong." White shame has now been embedded in the child's psyche.

The greatest way to heal from shame is to do the thing that feels the most shameful: name it, talk about it, shine the light of public knowing about it. But the public collective prefers that Whiteness remains invisible, especially to White people. Thus, White trauma is born, even as Whiteness, among the collective, is not the victim.

The construct of American individualism creates a lush and nutritious landscape in which fear, guilt, and shame can flourish. The image of the bootstrap, do-it-yourself, individual exceptionalism of our culture in the United States keeps us isolated from the collective. We don't recognize our interconnectedness, which allows not just our fear, guilt, and shame to be perpetuated, but also our bad behavior. We can continue to practice the violence of Whiteness, constantly retraumatizing not only BIPOC but also ourselves, in our own happy little bubbles, and remain unaware of the ways in which these emotions are in operation in our psyches. To be "ruggedly individualistic" often means to separate ourselves from the full emotional experience of being human—we can see this in the ways in which toxic masculinity suppresses men's ability to express sadness, grief, and even sometimes love as anything other than anger. The competitive nature of our values means that there must always be a winner, which means there are also "losers," rather than a cohesive collective working together for the good of all. To be White is to constantly be striving for an impossible goal and never actually attain it, while at the same time to separate from the truth of our own selves, rendering us unable to operate in the collective, requiring silent self-betrayal, and retraumatizing us over and over again.

When we examine the symptoms of trauma, we can begin to recognize the ways they manifest in Whiteness. Mohamed states that "in various formulations, trauma is described as 'a blockage,' 'anti-narrative,' or a 'violent event [that] occur[s] as an absolute inability to know it.'" She goes on to say,

> These interpretations of trauma call for subjects to reclaim their voices in order to transform traumatic experiences into experiences that are incorporated into one's consciousness and thereby freed of their painful symptoms. They demand also that wider audiences recall and acknowledge the source of the trauma. To cure the trauma and transform it into a lived experience, one that is controlled in memory rather than controlling, it must be recognized, made legible, spoken of, heard.[7]

In other words, for White trauma to be healed, it must be brought out into the open, examined, dissected, and given voice. When pastoral care is offered to White congregants, it might be helpful—at times, when appropriate—to help your congregants understand how the values and constructs of Whiteness are at play in their own psyches in damaging ways, creating undue pressure and tension. Then, you can help them resist it as an act of their own healing.

BIPOC TRAUMA

While White trauma is rendered virtually invisible to the White people who carry it, the BIPOC community deals with micro- and macroaggressions daily. LePera astutely points out that the ACEs (Adverse Childhood Experiences) test—a standard psychological tool to identify trauma—doesn't have a single question about obvious overt racism, much less the subtler and more pervasive forms of racism that BIPOC experience every day. "When you live in a world that is unsupportive and outright threatening—in the education system, prison system, health care system, and most workplaces—you are existing in an almost constant state of trauma." Dealing with these stressors at both individual and institutional levels "may place [marginalized groups] squarely into 'a state of relative helplessness,'" which is the essential definition of trauma.[8]

If you're White, it's very important for you to remember this when offering care to the BIPOC community, because it's an experience to which you cannot relate. Even if you have had an experience you think is similar, you still can't fully understand. It's also really important to check your Whiteness when working with BIPOC because our Whiteness often wants to offer justifications for other White people's bad behavior, and if we offer those justifications to BIPOC when they are sharing an experience with us, we are straight-up perpetuating harm and retraumatizing them. Very often, interpersonal interactions are layered and nuanced, and as White people, we need to understand that BIPOC experience a racialized nuance that often flies right past our consciousness, but it's there doing harm to them all the time. We need to be willing to recognize this, acknowledge it, and believe marginalized communities when they tell us it's happening—especially in the context of pastoral care, because we can do so much damage within that context if we are not carefully practicing agency over our own Whiteness.

WHAT THEY REALLY MEAN BY "ANGRY BLACK WOMAN"
(Josh)

Earlier in my career, I accepted the role of outreach pastor for a fledgling, predominantly White inner-city church. During those first few weeks there, I spent many hours getting as much info on the community and the congregation as I could. I received an overwhelming amount of information and history about the church. Another staff member and I devoted much time to wandering the neighborhood, connecting with parishioners who lived nearby. Toward the end of my first week, he gave me one piece of advice that stuck out: "As best as you can, avoid Ms. V."

"Who is Ms. V, and why should I avoid her?" I asked. I assumed Ms. V was a local woman at odds with the church, maybe angry over the gentrifying neighborhood. Perhaps she was a racist, and my colleague was looking out for me. He gave a sort of piecemeal description. "She has not liked any of our previous hires; she's tough to deal with, a bit aggressive and mean. . . . She's a member but does not like it here and won't leave." His answer was cryptic, vague, and unclear about what made this woman "mean." My own biases reinforced an image of an old racist White woman. I mentally prepared for a future encounter with this supposedly angry, bitter woman.

A few Sundays later, a Black woman approached me and introduced herself as the infamous Ms. V. She exuded a warm personality and the familiar hospitality that occurs when two Black people meet in a sea of White folks. I couldn't quite clock her age, but since Black doesn't crack, I assumed she must be somewhere above middle age. I struggled to see how she could be the same "angry old woman" I was supposed to avoid—our brief encounter was a stark difference from what I had been warned about.

She thanked me for coming to the community and told me she was excited to have another person of color working with her in the church. When we locked eyes, I saw the look of pride from her—the same look I have seen elders give to me and others in my age group. It's the look of pride and joy found in the hope of the up-and-coming generation, and it let me know her introduction and words of encouragement were genuine and authentic. Its authenticity caused me to question the narrative I'd received about her, and while I knew how often Black women are typecast into the character of "angry Black woman," I struggled to accept that this colleague would have done that. I thought he was different, more conscious than other church leaders. After all, he was one of the people who hired me, and he wanted to build a diverse neighborhood church.

Having noticed my interaction with Ms. V, my colleague caught me after service to let me know that whatever I did or said left a good impression. Ms. V had told him how excited she was to have me be part of the church. While I smiled and pretended that I had just achieved something, I swallowed back the creeping sense of awareness in my gut. Ms. V was not, in fact, angry or mean, but she was Black. Her Blackness meant she would not need to do anything to be perceived as angry or aggressive to the White leadership of the church. I was not told to avoid her because of her anger, but because her Blackness was too loud.

I made it a point to connect with her on Sunday mornings and learned why she joined the church. She was hooked by the vision of the church the same way I was. A few years before my arrival, she was sold a vision of a diverse inner-city church centered on racial reconciliation. She bought in and joined the church. But the ingrained **misogynoir** of the congregation and its leadership never made space for her capacity to serve. Outside of the church, she was a single mother and sat on several nonprofit boards and advised other churches on their outreach efforts. She was an incredible leader and advocate for the community. But within the walls of the church, leadership did not view her with that level of competency.

The pain of the microaggressions she experienced in the church and the weight of the larger systemic trauma that she carried were viewed as theater and mere misplaced emotions. When she shared her experiences she was met with eye rolls and folded arms; her emotions were considered unwarranted and overly dramatic. The rightful frustration she felt from being sold a false vision of the church was perceived as aggression and forcefully quieted. Ms. V was never granted the authority to lead that White congregants of lesser credentials were given. When she raised her voice to call out the blatant marginalization, she was treated like a pariah and not a full congregational member.

With nearly every pastor or church I coach or consult, we run into the problem of the *angry Black woman*, but neither Black women nor their anger is the actual problem in these scenarios. Pastors lament these women like Paul's thorn in the side. They vent about the anger or frustration from Black women and other women of color as if these women should be thankful and appreciative that racism is even being discussed. Instead of doing the necessary self-reflection to see where Whiteness is at play, these pastors reinforce the interlocking harm of racism and sexism.

In March 2021, author Rebeca Traister was speaking on the *Ezra Klein Show* podcast. Her topic was how our culture responds to leadership, particularly how we as a society respond to White men who exhibit traits of dominance and abuse. Her incredible commentary on leadership beautifully articulated what I see happening within pastoral care. During the conversation, host Ezra Klein brought up Steve Jobs. According to many writers who followed him, Jobs was extremely difficult to deal with as a person. His toxic behavior in the workplace and within his family life is often regarded as the cost of his greatness and innovation. Traister interrogated this idea, stating:

> This is one of the costs of a long history of having understood white men as fully human in a way that we don't understand other people as being fully human. We have been able to imaginatively integrate when it comes to white men their weaknesses, their faults, their failings, their cruelty as part of their complex humanity, because white men have been presented to us in our literature and in our culture and through the ways that we've configured family and politics and law, white men have been presented to us as fully human, containing contradiction and complexity.[9]

This thoughtful reflection by Traister echoes much of what I have seen in efforts of pastoral care—and not just regarding issues of leadership. It's about who is perceived as fully human and thus given space to express a full range of emotions and feelings. In pastoral care, White folks and White men, in particular, have more of their perceived needs met because they are seen as fully human. They are given grace as complex beings who are still coming along or figuring it out, while Black congregants—and Black women in particular—often have their tone policed before being heard and are asked not to present anger or any high level of emotion. When they show a justifiable level of anger or grief, they are defined by those emotions only, and the cause of those emotions is never interrogated. Black and Brown women like Ms. V are routinely gaslit for demanding to be treated and cared for with the same level of intentionality as their White peers and congregants.

White pastors often let White (usually male) congregants express their anger in harmful or destructive ways and call it passion, but this comes at the expense of creating safety for BIPOC. This often looks like pastoral leadership turning their head while men operate out of their toxic masculinity. Their behavior and treatment of women and women of color is then explained away or even justified. Simultaneously, the emotions and pain from racially traumatizing experiences and gender discrimination for BIPOC are considered a threat and quieted.

For years, Ms. V worked quietly to get the church to address its racism. She was set aside and only received feedback when she raised her voice, demanding to be heard like White congregants were. The result was that she was labeled as angry, bitter, and aggressive, and treated as an outsider. By the time I had arrived on staff she was treated like a threat and not part of the community. Her emotions and needs could not be treated equally to those of her White counterparts because she was not seen as fully human and thus could not be viewed as a fully integrated person within congregational life. The pastor's tool kit only knew how to silence the raised voice of BIPOC and not take care of the wounds caused within congregational life. I would learn this lesson all too well when I decided to leave the church because of a similar level of gaslighting and microaggression Ms. V had been experiencing for years.

Get Out

If you're a reader who is BIPOC, queer, gender nonconforming, differently abled, or a combination of any of these identities, you do not have to suffer under a system of pastoral care that chooses to uphold oppression instead of your flourishing. If you're gaslit or tone-policed in the face of racism or misogyny, it may be time to leave. If your pastoral care team does not have the tools to care for your identities' particularities, it is OK to go.

God did not call you to suffer like this. It took me a long time to realize this—much longer than I care to admit, primarily because I was socialized to accept a form of pastoral care that placed my needs behind those of White folks. My experiences, perspectives, and longings had to fit within the White gaze to have credibility. I was used to leadership that didn't have to accept the complexity of my full humanity and all the nuance that came with it. I settled for an idea of belonging that allowed me to appear present even as I was not valued. This type of suffering lacked any real redemptive value. It simply reinforced a racist idea of where I fit in the world. This does not have to be marginalized readers' experience; please hear me when I say this: There's freedom on the other side of that transition. It may hurt like hell, but getting out is liberation.

If you're a White pastor or leader and want to do whatever you can to avoid vulnerable identities feeling what I'm talking about, you'll need to take the tools Kerry offers. You will also need to listen deeply to your congregation's vulnerable members and learn what it means for them to belong, what is necessary for them to feel fully human in your congregation, fully alive, fully welcomed. You need to wrestle with how your church allows certain people to take up more space than others. If you can do this task and accept all the emotion, nuance, and complexity that comes with it and commit to bringing it to reality? You'll be heading in a good direction.

ASSESSMENT 9.1: PASTORAL CARE

1. Now that you better understand both the values of Whiteness and the symptoms of trauma, can you think of how symptoms of White trauma may have manifested in yourself? What about those in your care?
2. If you have ever counseled members of the BIPOC community, how did the trauma of their marginalization contribute to their need for pastoral care? Were you aware of it at the time or is it only in retrospect that you can see it?
3. In what ways does White wounding manifest in your daily operations? Your lay leaders? Your congregants?
4. In what ways can you incorporate your understanding of racial trauma into your care practices?
5. How does an understanding of the treatment of Whiteness as an urgent matter of pastoral care change the way you will lead and care for your congregation corporately?
6. How is your church supporting the particular pastoral care needs of BIPOC, LGBT, queer, and gender nonconforming folks in the congregation?
7. How does your church address incidents of racism or microaggressions?
8. How do the voices of BIPOC in your congregation shape your imagination for belonging and care?
9. If your church had BIPOC who have left in the last few years, did you identify why they left? What steps will you take to reconcile pain or trauma caused in your congregation to those who left?

10

Modeling Interracial Dialogue

We've journeyed through quite a lot of material together. In this final chapter, we're going to do something a little different. Racial conversations—especially racial conversations between White people and BIPOC—can make White people really uncomfortable, but if you're going to commit to racial justice in your organization, you're about to start having them on the regular. We thought it would be helpful to model a healthy racial conversation for you, so Josh, Bry, and I hopped on a Zoom call to discuss some of the issues we've talked about throughout the book. You'll find a transcript of that conversation below; it's highly edited for length and clarity. If you'd like to watch the whole video for yourself, you can find it on my website at www.kerryconnelly.com/talk-with-josh-and-bry.

After that conversation, you'll find a template guide you can use to begin to develop your own strategy and action item list for making the changes we've discussed throughout this book. Remember, it won't happen overnight—this will be an investment of time, energy, and probably some tears. It's worth it. I promise.

The church has much to repent and lament. But the church is very much about redemption. Sunday doesn't come before the pain of Friday or the deep grief of Saturday, but it does, indeed, come. If you're willing to walk through that weekend with us, I believe the church can be an instigator of holy change in the world.

RACIAL IDENTITY FORMATION

Bryana: My first question is for Josh. What are the narratives around your racial identity that were shared with you when you were growing up, and how do you help other BIPOC work through their own racial identity development in the work you do today?

Josh: I wish I could answer that easily. As a biracial Black person, there was a slew of messages, both explicitly and implicitly, intentional and unintentional, about who I was and what it meant to have the body that I have—the features of my body, my hair, and my skin.

There was this sort of light-skinned privilege space. The texture of my hair, the tonality of my skin was something that both a lot of the Black folks and White folks that I was around sought after and desired and longed for. I didn't have that same longing because of the narratives around what it meant to be Black and what it meant to be White. In my adolescent years, I really struggled to feel I was "Black enough." And I know a lot of biracial people, even some, you know, Black people who are not biracial feel that tension.

Much of that came from too narrow [a definition] of what it meant to be Black, too narrow a scope of what Blackness was. It wasn't [just] hip-hop, it wasn't sports. The White spaces that I was in were perpetuating those same messages.

In middle school, one of the few Black kids in my high school started a rumor that I was Latino. I cornered him in the hallway one day. I was like, "Why would you make this up about me?" He said, "Bro, you too smart to be Black." He himself, being Black, believed that there's no way someone of intelligence could also be a Black person.

So, when I work with other BIPOC, we start there, with [the question of] what narratives did you hear growing up? What narratives are about your body and live inside your body? These kinds of racial ideas are manifested (in) a very embodied way.

Kerry: Interrogating narratives is so important. To interrogate narratives and say, is that true? Is that the only perspective? It's so important.

I have a question for you, Bry. In chapter 1, you talk about digging deep into a critical family history. I know you've embarked on this journey a little bit yourself. Can you talk a little bit about where you're at on that journey?

Bryana: When we think about the anti-Blackness narratives that even we as biracial and Black people inherit or are victim to, the critical family history takes it a little bit of a step further, and it's less about tracing your family roots back however many generations, but tracing and understanding their racial identity development and their understanding of race and their identity, the identity that they used, if you will, to survive depending on the generation that they lived in. It really takes a critical look at how the movement of our relatives and what's going on politically, socially, culturally in their time impact their racial identity and what they claim.

Kerry: It's so important for White people, and really eye-opening, when they start to look at what their racial family history is. They might start to notice when they actually became White. Because maybe if they were immigrants, they weren't always White. My family was not always considered White because they came over during the Irish emigration.

They definitely experienced certain [exclusionary] things, but then they assimilated into Whiteness and became White and then took on many of the racist belief systems that would help them maintain that Whiteness. And because of their skin color they were able to do it in just one generation.

Bryana: That's so powerful!

Kerry: It's powerful to understand that and to recognize how it's in operation in your own lineage, and in your own family and in the narratives that your family passes down, to perpetuate racism in order to protect our own assimilation into Whiteness. Right?

Bryana: Absolutely! I kind of did that for myself as a way to feel closer to my African American roots, to better understand where I came from. I have a whole new appreciation for the way that my family had to survive and to live in the midst of the civil rights era. So, I think for BIPOC folk, it's also a really important exercise to do, just to understand, and to connect to our roots.

THE WHITE MOVE TO INNOCENCE

Josh: Kerry, I'm thinking you just named something that really cuts off what some people might have used as a move to innocence. That's something that I've seen you do quite a few times—not pivoting the way a lot of White folks do, to move to innocence, believing it to be a way to remove themselves from being racist. I would love to hear how you're thinking about that, and what it means for White folks to not just make a move to innocence, but to actually divest from power. And what steps need to be taken to actually divest from power? Do you see that becoming a performative action in others or even within yourself?

Kerry: Well, yeah, sure. I always feel that within myself. If I'm going to be real, that's the first instinct, to be defensive. The other thing I have to completely confess is that, very often when I am called out or confronted with something that I have said or done where my Whiteness has come out to play, I want to run to all my Black friends and have them tell me how good I am, and I really need to practice agency over it. In other words, I need to resist that initial urge and consider my actions before I rush in and do something stupid and harmful.

But the question that you're really asking is about how White people can divest ourselves of power.

It's always going to be contextual. You have to be willing to look at a situation and recognize where you have the power, and how can you divest it? Is it by not taking up all the space in the room? Is it not using up the mic all the time? Is it simply being the person who provides financial resources and not direction? Not being the boss, but rather providing resources to people who may be underresourced, but not undertalented by any stretch of the imagination, right? So, it's recognizing where you hold the power and then how you can divest yourself of that power. But you have to be aware of the dynamic, of where the power is. Sometimes it's subtle.

REPRESENTATION WITHOUT TOKENISM

Kerry: I have a question for both of you that is super real. Let's say I'm a pastor of a predominantly White church, and we are hoping to put together an anti-racism task force. I know we want BIPOC voices leading that initiative. How can I invite Black and Brown-skinned people in a way that is not harmful? In a way that authentically invites you into a leadership role, but without doing harm?

Bryana: Ooh, that's a loaded question.

Kerry: I know! I also want to acknowledge too that you're not a monolith. You guys are not sitting here speaking for all of the entire population of BIPOC.

Bryana: That's where I was going to start. And the work can't be dependent on the few Black and or Brown people in your congregation.

Don't burden them to hold all the answers and to lead, but approach it as a way for you to learn and to invite them into the conversation. Don't assume that because they are Black or Brown, that they even want to engage in such a task force.

Understanding Whiteness as a first step and hiring experts or connecting with White people who have done that work—instead of going to Black and Brown folks—is an important first step.

Josh: I had a conversation where somebody said if a church wanted to diversify, they could just hire a person of color in order to have leadership that reflects where you're going. That's just not true.

I've been the person of color in that situation, and it does not work out that way. The question is, what do you intend to be the outcome by putting that person in a position of leadership? How do you plan to empower them in a unique and particular way?

How do you plan to ensure their safety—knowing that leadership of any kind is risky and dangerous, you're putting someone in leadership who can experience a unique type of harm? If you're not going to ensure that there are buffers around that person, support for that person when people start to push back and they become the lightning rods of the work, are you going to leave them out to dry or protect them?

Are these people being chosen [for the task force] just because they're the few people of color? Or are they equipped in some capacity to do this work? As Bry said, not every person of color is equipped to lead this conversation. There are other skills that have to be there. And if those aren't there, then it's time to look for somebody outside of this space. I think churches really struggle with the capacity to listen to voices that are outside their four walls or outside their theological scope.

[We only want people who] fit in our theological box, who are safe to come in and share with us. But sometimes you've got to disrupt that space in order to actually get at what God has been doing and how God is moving. And regardless of whether it's race, gender, or sexuality, your church does not hold all the answers. God is already at work outside of the space that you're in. You don't have that market cornered. So, when we cut ourselves off from that, and we don't allow other voices to inhabit our space with us, not only are we not expressing the hospitality of God, but we're also not able to embody some of the richness and nuance of the spirit of God, which is deeply needed to do this conversation well.

PERFORMATIVE JUSTICE AND SAFE SPACES FOR BIPOC

Kerry: I want to understand too what kinds of actions should I engage in or not engage in that would help make you feel safe?

Bryana: When there's only a couple of Black and Brown folks, it's safe to recognize that it is not a safe space for Black and Brown folks when they are in the racial minority.

It's hard to find a perfect word that would help someone feel safe when they're in a situation already where they're just not. But I do think one of the characteristics of a White supremacist culture is perfectionism. [One of the best things you can do is] recognizing that you are probably going to mess up and you probably are going to say the wrong thing and to be open about that with that person to say, "Hey, I know I have a lot to learn, but I want to make sure whatever work that we do is not harmful. I am open always to feedback and for honesty on ways that I can be less harmful in whether that's my words or my actions."

Josh, I think there's a paradox for some White folks who really want to do this work of anti-racism, a sort of damned if you do and damned if you don't. For example, they're told to elevate or amplify BIPOC voices. So, they put them on websites and brochures, but then they get messages of how that's inappropriate.

So how can churches balance this in a way that doesn't do harm and actually is an act of anti-racism? Is that even possible?

Josh: I want us to investigate and dig deep as to why we made that move. I would guess that decision is made because we want to have an external presentation of something that's not true within the life of the congregation. It is easy to change a picture on our website. It is harder to investigate our theological treatises and start using Black and Brown theologies. Instead of challenging our all-White theological structure, it is easier to have a brochure with a smiling Black child that might be a recipient of some church outreach program. It is harder for the worship team to step back and say, we are going to play music differently and switch to maybe a bilingual format.

A lot of the moves we make that try to communicate anti-racism are easy. They don't require any real challenges. The work of anti-racism is about adaptive change. What we're really inviting folks to do is take a deeper look at the culture of the organization and say, why is it that these things are White? How did this come to be? And if we are to change it, what needs to happen? And that gets to some deeper, bedrock levels of our cultural narrative and beliefs, and that's where the real work starts to happen. So, I think it's possible. I don't think it happens without stumbling over ourselves and repeatedly making mistakes, which folks have a hard time doing, but also, being open to being held accountable. Especially after the murder of George Floyd, there were so many moves toward being involved, but there was no accountability to ensure that that work continued or had any value in and of itself.

Bryana: There was a lot of performative allyship or performative work happening.

Josh: I know a lot of people that were doing it because it was the trendy thing to do. And you start asking people why, who told you to do this? And they couldn't actually identify it. For a lot of churches when we start really getting into the receipts of their work, and we said, who told you to do this? There wasn't anyone of any kind of wisdom or expertise or experience or interest in this work, just what [they] saw other people doing. But they hadn't actually addressed the ways in which they had consistently harmed Black and Brown folks in their congregation. So again, who told you all to do this? 'Cause it wasn't the people in your church and you haven't done anything to help those people who are hurting and that you caused harm to.

WHITE CONCEPTS OF THE DIVINE

Josh: Bry, you brought up a lot of that in this book, talking about your experiences growing up in a White church context, and that testimony was beautiful and helpful. I would love to hear more about how that shaped your spirituality.

Bryana: I would say it's a journey, not a destination. I wouldn't say I've arrived at a certain place yet. I continue to evolve and to grow. But growing up in a predominantly White church and worshiping in predominantly White spaces really did impact my understanding of the Divine, in a way that, for the longest time, wasn't something that was in my consciousness.

As I got older and I started more consciously recognizing, wait a minute, if the Divine is White and if the Divine is male and if the Divine is blue eyes and straight hair, I don't see any of me in that.

I don't see my father in that. So, what does that do for my whole understanding of myself, my value, my self-worth? It now makes me so passionate about making sure when we talk about this in the chapters about children and raising children in the church, you know, we've got to take care of our babies.

We've got to take care of our White babies, our Black babies, and our Brown babies. They need to understand that Jesus and justice are one and the same. And they need to see themselves represented in all kinds of images and explanations of the Divine. If we're to create a future generation that does true good in the world, that is foundational.

ON BEING "TOO POLITICAL"

Bryana: Kerry, when you are coaching White pastors, how do you address a common fear of upsetting congregation members or impacting church numbers by being too political?

Kerry: The bottom line, there's no way to sugarcoat it. There is going to be a cost and they're probably going to lose members and that needs to be OK. It's not going to be nice and neat and clean. They're not going to be able to do it without making some people uncomfortable, first and foremost themselves. The Bible is highly political. Jesus was highly political. That is part of the cost of the work. But I also think that it's important to understand that the crucifixion was horrific, but resurrection is beautiful, right? I believe a resurrection is on the other side of what this painful journey encompasses. This is the work that we need to do and it's going to suck.

And that's OK because it's worth it.

For White leaders doing this work, it's important to understand that there's always going to be somebody pissed off at you. The most important thing that I can remember is to stay in my lane, and my lane is companioning other White people through the deconstruction of their Whiteness. I don't get to co-opt the Black experience for my racial work. My work is to confront Whiteness in myself and to help companion other White people as they confront it in themselves. That's an important distinction. Because sometimes White people come into this work saying, oh my gosh, we have to help the Black people. And I'm saying, no, *we* are the ones who need healing. It's us that needs repair. It's us who have a wound that needs the touch of the Divine, and to be healed, right? That's a paradigm shift that White people need to make, especially if you're a White person who wants to lead an organization into anti-racism work, you have to be willing to rip open your shirt and show the wounds a little bit, and that's not fun.

Bryana: When you said that you weren't here to co-opt the Black experience. That's deep.

Kerry: I think a lot of White people want to do that, you know? And I have to even practice agency over it because I care about my best friend Aisha, for example. We share a tattoo. She's family. My kids have her number on speed dial. I want to share her stories, but they're not mine to share. I have to be really, really careful about not co-opting her experience. It's got to be about examining my own self.

RACISM IS DIVISIVE; ANTI-RACISM IS NOT

Josh: Kerry, you said churches are going to lose people doing this work. A lot of churches think that anything that will create division is wrong. Can you talk about the practice of communal discernment and listening, and activating the 80 percent that is either on board or willing to be swayed? How do you walk people through that?

Kerry: I do think that that is a leadership skill. First, pastors need to be thinking about deconstructing Whiteness as an urgent matter of pastoral care for White people. The more White people who do this work, the closer we'll be to healing the racial divide in our country, the closer we'll be to the point where we are not doing harm. And the first step in that is healing the White wounds.

It's not going to happen overnight. You're not just going to hire a consultant and everything's going to be fixed. It's an investment in relationship, in time spent with people and journeying with them.

Sometimes that's sitting down with a person to say, "Hey, your behavior was painful. It was harmful. You did harm to people," and have that kind of pastoral conversation. And then with other people, it's going to be [saying], "Hey, I'm here in relationship with you. I love you. And we need to work through this together." It's never about attacking people. We're interrogating narratives and everybody's feelings are always valid. The perspectives feeding them may not be. That's what I try to help people understand.

I get that it really sucks to be called out for doing or saying something racist. But what's the perspective that's feeding those emotions? For example, what makes you feel that was a personal attack on you, rather than an interrogation of the narratives that you are embodying? Let's try to shift your perspective and then maybe see if your feelings change. All of that takes investment. It takes a willingness to show up in relationship. And again, it's messy because people are messy. Humans are messy. But that's how I approach that.

PARTNERSHIPS BETWEEN BLACK AND WHITE CHURCHES

Kerry: Bry, in chapter 5, you mentioned the Black church, and I know you have experience with White churches wanting to partner with a Black church. Can you talk about that kind of a relationship and what could work and (what could) go really, really wrong?

Bryana: I think that kind of a relationship can be healthy when the White church has already done the work, individually and collectively as a church. I would ask if the White church has interrogated Whiteness? Have you interrogated the ways in which your practices and your culture are harmful to the BIPOC population? It's healthy when the White church has done that work and they want relationship and a mutually beneficial relationship. It's harmful if this is the first time the White church is engaging with Black people outside of their own congregation.

That's when it ends up being [interracial] book studies and video discussions full of White people, waking up to their Whiteness and the harsh realities and lived experiences of Black people. Just watching videos that talk about violence against Black folks or racism is harmful to BIPOC. There's often White guilt that shows up and White tears. And there's an expectation now that the Black community has to hold and to carry that burden of that awakening, which again, could be a further trauma to the Black congregation. [That's] not a mutually beneficial relationship—it's a consuming relationship. And that can be very harmful and traumatic.

Kerry: So often in those relationships, the assumption is that the White church is there to help the Black church, and there's never the assumption that the White church has a need, and that the Black church can minister to them. Can you talk a little bit about that?

Bryana: You're exactly right. It becomes, we're here to save you. We're here to help you. In the context of a White congregation in relationship with a Black congregation without doing the work first, it's the "poor Black people" mentality.

Josh: For me the question is, how do we build those collaborative spaces? There is ingrained in our language and our pedagogy a belief in the superiority of Whiteness.

We have to really sit and think about the ways in which we're perpetuating some of those things as congregations. How people in our congregation are going to view the cultural practices, the liturgical practices, the theological practices of a White church with a greater degree of authority than the Black church practices.

Kerry: That is a brilliant point. A key part of deconstructing Whiteness is how much do I center Whiteness? How much is my Whiteness, my normalized view, the lens that I see everything through? And the thing that I'm going to say to White people who maybe don't want to hear this, is that a lot of times we are going to have to have that pointed out to us by our BIPOC siblings. Because we just can't see it. I hope that when it is pointed out to us, we can respond with grace and gratitude rather than with defensiveness and obnoxious White tears.

BIPOC-ONLY SPACES

Kerry: I really want to understand or explore a little bit more the importance of BIPOC-only spaces and why they are so important.

Josh: God is interested in the uniqueness and the complexity and nuance of our individual lives. And if we, as a community of faith, want to reflect the divine life, then we have to be interested in attending to the unique particularities, nuance, and complexity as a people in our congregations' lives, that also includes their racial identity. That means that as White folks, you do not have all the tools to meet everyone's needs, which means if you want to care for the particularities, uniqueness, and complexity of BIPOC, you have to also be aware of things you cannot provide to those nuances.

If I cannot provide them, then how do I make space for somebody else to, how do I make space just as the divine life has made space for us to be in a relationship, for those particular areas to be nurtured, cared for, attended to so that when we come together again, there is an ability to bring one's full self present.

This is a way we get to make space for someone in a really holy and profound way.

BEING A GOOD WHITE FRIEND

Josh: So, last question. And this is one of my favorite questions. Kerry, I am interested as to how you as a White person hold yourself accountable in this work; to whom or to what are you accountable?

Kerry: I think it's really important for me to respect the BIPOC people I love by not going to them immediately with racialized questions. I do have a small group of White people who are trained and dedicated to this work. When I have an issue, I will seek out the counsel of my White friends and depending on the strength of my own emotional response, the longer it will be before I will bring it to one of my friends of color. Because I want to make sure that I'm not just vomiting all of my emotions onto these people that I care about, but it is still important for me to get objective feedback from the BIPOC community.

When I feel I'm in a healthy place and I can do it well and without harm, I will say, "If you have the time, the willingness, the desire, and the energy to do so, would you be willing to have a conversation with me about a racial experience that I had, and help me see my own Whiteness?" I also tell them no is a complete answer and a perfectly acceptable response. Because they don't owe me anything—they don't owe me a conversation around this stuff.

Usually, my friends tend to be pretty honest with me, which is both a blessing and a curse and I'm only half-joking. I'm very blessed to have friends who are honest with me about these things.

I try to be quick to apologize. When I mess up on social media, I leave my mistakes up so that other people can learn from it. I don't take it down because that just keeps me looking nice and pristine. And, that's not the truth. I leave the post up so everybody can go to my Facebook page and read it. So that's how I do it.

Josh: Can I ask a follow-up question? This idea of friendship is one of mutuality and reciprocity, but having been on the [metaphorical] works-cited page of many White people as their "Black friend," without consenting to that, can you talk about how you define a friendship?

Because I think there are going to be a lot of readers who are going to say, yes, I have Black friends and I let them hold me accountable, or I reach out to them and say, Hey, will you look at this or check this out. But without having done any of the necessary work to frame what that relationship actually looks like.

Kerry: That's a really great question. I honestly don't think it's fair for me as a White person to consider myself in deep relationship with a Black person unless we've had a conversation around race and preferably a conversation in which they may have had to confront me with something.

I feel that's almost a benchmark for real relationship because here's what I know: As a White person entering into a relationship with a person of color, the work is mine to earn their trust, to demonstrate my trustworthiness. Not that I will always get it right, but that I am aware of the ways in which I might do harm, just because of my embodiment. So, I try to be really, really aware of that.

Bryana: If you are a White person and have a BIPOC friend and have never had a conversation about race, I think that's worth interrogating in and of itself. It's not safe to assume as a White person that if you are friends with a BIPOC and you've never talked about race, it's because they just don't want to, because the question is, are they comfortable enough with you to do that?

Josh: My fear and the thing that I've seen play out so often is that people hear that and think, I check all those boxes, I texted my Black friend during the George Floyd protest and asked how they were doing, they said they are doing pretty shitty. So they think, we had a conversation on race. Kerry, you gave very tangible examples of mutuality. "Can you look at this? Can you reflect on this, can you review this?"

What's missing in a lot of these contexts is mutuality and reciprocity. I remember when I first started doing ministry and very quickly became the Black ministry friend of a bunch of men twice my age.

I didn't feel I had an agency to consent to that relationship. And yet I was being cited as "my Black friend, Josh." We have to also consider how we have power over people. Do they really get to consent to that? What is that relationship built on? Is it mutuality and reciprocity and have both parties agreed to what that actually looks like in motion?

Kerry: Thank you for pointing that out. And I want to even expand a little bit more about the agency issue, because I've done it. I tell a really painful story about it in *Good White Racist?* Oh, it's so painful. And so public. But it taught me such a good lesson.

White people tend to do this thing where we just assume that because we're being nice that all the Black people in the room want to be friends with us. And we assume relationality really fast. I try to remember that just because I know I wrote a book about racial justice doesn't mean that the next Black person that I meet knows that I'm safe and feels safe with me, right? And wants to automatically be my friend. And guess what, as a completely separate human from me they get to have self-agency and decide all for themselves whether they want to be in relationship with me or not. It's not just up to me, you know? So you're talking about self-agency and mutuality and reciprocity and it's such an important aspect of friendship that I don't think White people really understand, especially the power, just the power of our [White] embodiment and what it brings into an interracial friendship, that there's an embodied power just right there. That makes me inherently unsafe for my friends. And I need to do the work. The work is mine to do, to prove myself trustworthy.

Conclusion
Your Plan of Action

It's time to get to work. You're equipped with knowledge and understanding, and now it's time to create your strategy and put it into practice. Using what you've learned from the previous chapters, answer the questions in this section. When you're done, you should have an actionable plan that you can follow to keep you on task and clear on what your next steps are.

YOUR ANTI-RACIST ACCOUNTABILITY TEAM (ARAT)

Most churches work by committee, and yours may want to develop a team dedicated to implementing this strategy. That's great, but if you were reading carefully, you know that these types of committees are fodder for a lot of problematic and performative justice. Make sure you can check ALL of the boxes below before you ask a group of people to commit time and energy to this project.

___ If the lead pastor is not part of this committee, they have agreed to actively participate in monthly meetings. (Hint: They should be part of the committee.)

___ The committee has been authorized and empowered to make actionable decisions.

___ Resources have been set aside for this committee—outside of the basement. This includes financial resources.

___ The people on the committee have been vetted and are not only passionate but well equipped for this work. For example, they have training in conflict management, racial identity and awareness, and/or inherent bias.

___ If the people on the committee are not inherently equipped, resources have been set aside to train them. This includes getting outside consulting or training.

___ If necessary, we have identified and hired the appropriate consultant to guide us through this work.

___ BIPOC voices, from within the church or outside it, who are both willing and equipped to do this work are guiding the team. Unless we are paying them, their labor is done willingly and without expectation. The team is willing to submit to their leadership.

YOUR ANTI-RACIST VISION AND MISSION STATEMENT

Vision and mission statements are important because they help your congregation understand who you are and how you show up in the world. They act as a metric against which you can measure your work to ensure that it is aligned with and working toward your goals. To that end, it's important to have a vision and mission statement for your anti-racism work, to make it public, and to ultimately work it into your overall vision and mission statements. Then you can create an action plan that specifically works to move you closer to living out your mission and making your vision for the world a reality.

Key to doing this work is understanding the difference between a vision statement and mission statement. I've taken many leadership teams through vision and mission workshops, and this is how I always define it for them: A *vision statement* describes how you want the world to be. A *mission statement* tells us what you do to make it that way. For example, you might develop a vision and mission statement similar to this:

Our Vision

We envision a world in which racism is completely eradicated and all people are celebrated for their unique humanity, are able to flourish, and lean into the fullness of who God created them to be.

Our Mission

To be a church that represents the realm of God through radical welcome by divesting ourselves of power, resisting supremacy culture, and celebrating the full humanity of all who walk through our doors.

YOUR ACTIONABLE ITEMS

Each chapter asked important questions intended to help you dig deeper and identify ways in which pseudosupremacy is at work in your church. Now, for each chapter, identify specific changes that need to occur based on what you've discovered. Be clear about the problem and the proposed shift or change.

LEADERSHIP _____

_____

_____

_____

PREACHING AND LITURGY _____

_____

_____

_____

MUSIC _____

_____

_____

_____

SMALL GROUPS _____

_____

_____

_____

BUILDINGS AND GROUNDS_____

_____

_____

_____

COMMUNICATIONS _____

_____

_____

_____

MISSIONS AND SERVICE _____

_____

_____

_____

CHILDREN AND YOUTH_____

_____

_____

_____

PASTORAL CARE _____

_____

_____

_____

ROLES AND COMMUNICATIONS

Operational leadership teaches us that it's important for people on teams to know their responsibilities. We'll use the RACI role management model to help your team implement your action items.[1] The RACI chart will help you determine who is doing what by identifying who is responsible for carrying out tasks, who authorizes them, and who needs to be informed. It will help ensure that everyone knows what their responsibilities are, and it will help you think through who needs to be informed and consulted during this process.

Responsible: Who will actually implement the task or change.

Authorize/Accountable: Who has the power to greenlight a project and is ultimately responsible for its success.

Consulted: Who has important information useful to the project.

Informed: Who will be impacted by the decision or project and need to know about its consequences.

To be clear, your accountability team will be conducting audits and suggesting changes, but other people may be the ones who are carrying them out. The chart below is an example only—fill out your own accordingly.

Task	Carry out audit of all sections	Develop multilingual selections of worship music	Select anti-racist children's curriculum
Responsible	Anti-Racist Accountability Team (ARAT)	Worship director	Children's/youth pastor
Authorize/ Accountable	Lead pastor	ARAT	ARAT
Consulted	Executive team / board Children's pastor Worship director Community service director Buildings and grounds	Choir Congregation Children's pastor	ARAT
Informed	Congregation Lead pastor	Choir Congregation Lead pastor	Lead pastor Parents Worship director

KEY DATES AND MILESTONES

It's important to set deadlines for your goals, because without them, work tends to hover unfinished in the ether of our everyday lives. Setting start and end-goal dates for your projects relative to anti-racism will help make them actually happen. Use the following matrix to help you develop your dates (I've added two examples for your reference). Add as many columns as necessary. Project management software like Asana is also a great tool for this.

Project	Anti-racism mission statement	Volunteer training
Start Date	4/23/22	5/1/22
Milestone 1	Committee submits first draft by 5/23/22	Curriculum identified and approved 6/1/22
Milestone 2	Committee submits final draft for approval 6/1/22	Training begins 6/15/22
End Goal	New mission statement on all marketing collateral by 6/15/22	All volunteers trained 8/1/22

YOUR ONGOING REVIEW PROCESS

It's important to remember that anti-racism work is not a one-and-done kind of thing—it's ongoing. In some cases, processes will need to be put in place; for example, volunteer training will need to incorporate a regular anti-racist component for new team members. In other words, it needs to become part of your process. It's the same for things like social media and marketing. In other cases, you'll simply want to check in to monitor your progress. Consider the list below to ensure you are creating standard operating procedures for ongoing anti-racism work in these areas and try to think of any others that might also apply to you.

Volunteer training

Racial crisis response

Review of financial distributions

Pulpit review (whose voice is heard how often?)

Small-group review

Children and youth review

Social media feed

Building accessibility

Music and worship review

Congregational check-in

Special programs

Building accessibility

Liturgies

A FINAL NOTE

The journey you're about to embark on is not going to be easy—that's a promise. But it will be worth it. When Scripture tells us that we are to be in the world but not of it, I think this is what it's getting at, this work of being present to the world's complexities, but also being willing to make a radical difference. Healing the White wound is no easy task, and as an institution, the global Christian church has a lot to repent for. But I also believe that we as a church body can be the genesis of a beautiful change, if we are only willing to look at the truth of our own wounding and finally take responsibility for our own healing. The strategy I've outlined here is entirely incomplete—it requires you. Your labor, your thought, your participation. There is so much work to be done.

But I believe in you.

Glossary

acculturation. The process by which BIPOC assume the standards of the dominant White culture; this is also a process of racial trauma.

accomplice. A member of the dominant society who shows up in solidarity with BIPOC when there is a known risk.[1]

ally. A member of the dominant society who shows up in solidarity with BIPOC when it is convenient.[2]

anti-Blackness. A social dynamic that both devalues Blackness and Black culture and marginalizes Black people and the issues that impact them. Anti-Blackness can manifest as both overt racism and more subtle structural and systemic racism, specifically in the form of socioeconomic oppression.[3] Within society, anti-Blackness can show up in a preference for White beauty standards and a disregard for Black culture, intellect, and contributions to the arts and sciences. It can also show up in subtle interpersonal interactions that have real impact, such as hiring practices (interviews), medical appointments, school settings.

BIPOC. This acronym stands for "Black, Indigenous, and people of color," with the intent to include voices that haven't been heard. It is meant to call attention to an important understanding of the historical experiences of Black people, as different from Indigenous, and other people of color (POC). While the intent is inclusive, a criticism of the term is that it blends a number of historically marginalized groups together, as if their experiences were the same. A good rule of thumb is to be as specific as you can when talking about issues of race. For instance, if you are discussing why Hollywood should take greater steps for inclusion and diversity, BIPOC is an appropriate term. However, if you are raising issues about the lack of Native American representation in films, "POC" is not specific enough. Another example: when raising awareness about police brutality toward Black people, we need to say "Black" people rather than "POC."

coconspirator. A member of the dominant society who shows up in solidarity with BIPOC proactively and when there is a known risk, because they understand their own participation in BIPOC oppression.[4]

code switching. A communication practice by BIPOC to alter their language or tone to be more palatable or understandable to White listeners or peers. Because Whiteness prefers Standard American English, the burden is on

181

BIPOC to accommodate Whiteness by moving out of, for example, African American Vernacular English.

color-blind racism. The idea that only the absence of accounting for race will bring racial equality. Color-blind racism rejects all racial categorizations and record keeping and makes no distinctions based on race. It relies on the idea that race no longer matters and rejects policies that have been designed to address a legacy of structural discrimination.[5]

colorism. Discrimination that treats those with lighter skin more favorably than those with darker skin. This practice is a product of racism in the United States, in that it upholds the White standards of beauty and benefits White people in the institutions of oppression (media, medical world, etc.).

cost reduction. "A process involving changes in values (personal, social, economic) which reduces the pains incurred in meeting the demands of a powerful other." Cost reduction tendencies will generally "deepen and stabilize social relations over and above the condition of balance."[6]

cultural appropriation. "The unacknowledged or inappropriate adoption of the customs, practices, ideas, etc., of one people or society by members of another and typically more dominant people or society."[7]

culture. The norms, values, practices, patterns of communication, language, laws, customs, psychological processes, and meanings shared by a group of people in a given time and place.

divestment of power. The willing relinquishing of power, privilege, and resources by dominant identities for the good of the collective. It requires the redistribution of funds and other resources to BIPOC and other marginalized communities, and the submission of dominant identities to the leadership of those on the margins.

escalation path. A clearly defined and easily accessible process employees and volunteers—especially those of color—can follow in order to report microaggressions and other unhealthy, toxic, or abusive situations in the workplace. An anti-racist escalation path will ensure the safety of both the reporter's emotional well-being and their job security while holding the organization accountable for dismantling oppressive systems that create unhealthy environments.

exceptionalism. A paradigm that Whiteness uses to help it ignore inconvenient truths about its impact in the world by pointing to exceptions to the norm, or to propagate the idea that Whiteness is somehow superior.

food desert. A region where people have little access to healthy, wholesome food due to poverty or geographical distance.

gentrification. "The restoration and upgrading of deteriorated urban property by middle-class or affluent people, often resulting in the displacement of lower-income people. Gentrification is not simply the renovation or restoration of a neighborhood, it's high-contrast classism—smudging of cultural identity."[8]

good White racist. A person who paradoxically is both good and racist at the same time.

individualism. "The belief that we are each unique and outside the forces of socialization."[9]

intersectional. Coined by Kimberlé Crenshaw in 1989, this term identifies the ways in which gender and race interact to perpetuate oppression or discrimination. Originally deployed to explore the impact of discrimination on Black women, intersectionality has been expanded to include how other identities (gender, sexual orientation, nationality, etc.) interact and interlock to create privileges and oppression.

macroaggression. A large-scale act of oppression and/or prejudice against an entire demographic based on race, gender, able-bodiedness, sexual preference or identity, or nationality. Examples might include rampant anti-Asian sentiment during the COVID-19 pandemic or widespread xenophobia following the attacks on September 11, 2001.

microaggression. "A statement, action, or incident regarded as an instance of indirect, subtle, or unintentional discrimination against members of a marginalized group such as a racial or ethnic minority."[10]

misogynoir. The anti-Black racist misogyny that Black women experience.

paternalism/paternalistic. The way in which a dominant group strips agency and consent from a vulnerable group of people or community, in the belief that they know the best way to solve the community's challenges.

performative justice. Any public action undertaken by an individual or organization aligned with the dominant identity that creates the impression of progressive allyship but does nothing to create real change, redistribute power, or eliminate injustice. Performative justice can be completely superficial, but often it is a step in the right direction; its danger lies in the idea that the perpetrator will believe that it is in itself enough.

perpetrator trauma. The neutral psychological response of perpetrators to their own violent actions that displays all the symptoms of victim trauma, even as they are not victims.

place. The local geography, community, and culture within which an organization exists, and the history pertaining to them. For example, when we work to understand *place* we look at the history and nature of the land and its ecologies, and how that impacts the culture of the area. We look at the community and how our organization has interacted with it, and we might examine how the local culture impacts our organization and vice versa.

positionality. "The concept that our perspectives are based on our place in society. Positionality recognizes that where you stand in relation to others shapes what you can see and understand."[11]

racialized context/event. A racialized context or event is any space or event at which racial dynamics cause either inner or outer conflict, whether implicitly or explicitly. Microaggressions are examples of a racialized event. A racialized event can occur even if there are no BIPOC in the room—for example, when a White person tells a racist joke or promotes a racist stereotype.

racially innocuous. A person's self-defensive, self-protective habit of behaving in ways "that may soften their racial, ethnic, and cultural expression so as not to stand out."[12]

racist context/event. Any event or space in which racism is displayed, implicitly or explicitly, without being addressed, called out, and dismantled by a person or people who identify as White. If the racist act is confronted only by BIPOC, it is still a racist event or context because the work of anti-racism was left to be done by people of color. White silence is complicity, and complicity is racist.

redlining. In response to a 1933 housing shortage, the federal government started a program intended to provide housing to White middle- and lower-middle-class families while leaving African Americans and other people of color out of new suburban communities. Accomplished by a systemic refusal to insure mortgages in and near African American neighborhoods—the policy became known as redlining, because the areas were outlined in red on geographical maps.[13]

segregation. Legal and enforced separation of races that subjugated Black Americans to subcitizen status. Segregation intended to keep the racial hierarchy and ensure White pseudosupremacy.

socialization. "Systematic training into the norms of our culture . . . the process of learning the meanings and practices that enable us to make sense of and behave appropriately in that culture. . . . Our beliefs need not be inherently true to have very real consequences."[14]

space. Distance, proximity, and access, and the power dynamics that result from the ways in which these are used in an organization. An audit of the way space is used to perpetuate dominance, for example, might examine who is kept farthest from the center of power and access and for what reasons; we might wonder who has the most access and how that impacts their power and influence in the organization and in the community beyond.

systemic racism. The complex intersection of multiple institutional systems (for example, banking, real estate, health care, criminal justice, voting, or education, to name a few) that works to favor Whiteness and oppress BIPOC in real outcomes experienced in everyday life.

trauma. "A response to an experience that renders an individual unable to properly process that experience, which may result in symptoms such as flashbacks, nightmares, feelings of alienation, diminished empathy, or avoidance of reminders of the initial trauma."[15]

voluntourism. A form of tourism for profit in which travelers use performing local service as their rationale to visit a new context or community. Typically the communities that travelers visit are Black and Brown, and the visitors' presence does little to disrupt systemic oppression.

White culture. A collection of Western values and beliefs that give a higher priority to "rugged individualism, competition, action-orientation, hierarchical power structures, standard American English, linear and future time orientation, Judeo-Christianity, European history, Protestant work ethic, objective science, owning goods and property, the nuclear family unit, and European aesthetics."[16]

White grief. A valid and understandable emotional reaction that a White person experiences when they begin to understand the full impact of racism and their participation in racist systems. In contrast to White tears, White grief is a part of the racial deconstruction process and leads to lamentation, repentance, and reparation. White grief centers Whiteness within the self only to deconstruct it, while working interpersonally and societally to decenter Whiteness and dismantle the culture of White pseudosupremacy.

White guilt. A useless emotion usually associated with the beginning of White racial awakening: White people feel guilty for being born White. However, it does nothing to foster healing. Moving past White guilt toward White accountability (owning one's privilege and divesting oneself of power) is more useful.

White pseudosupremacy. The concept of White supremacy is false, and language can be a powerful way to perpetuate or resist oppression. This book uses "pseudo" in front of "supremacy" to make clear that there is nothing superior about Whiteness.

White-savior complex. The belief held primarily by Western White people that White people alone are best equipped to "'fix' the problems of struggling nations" or BIPOC communities, "without understanding their history, needs, or the region's current state of affairs."[17] The complex causes White people to completely disregard BIPOC wisdom and leadership, and rarely results in systemic change. Rather, it tends to perpetuate the perceived need for White assistance by maintaining the status quo.

White tears. The phenomenon in which White people, when confronted with their own racial behavior, express pain and hurt over being called out for it. The reaction often includes crying and horror at the implication of being called a racist. This behavior centers White feelings over the real impact and harm done by racism, and often places BIPOC in the uncomfortable position of having to comfort the White person displaying the emotion and reassure them that they are not actually racist. This is a manipulative and defensive posture that effectively shuts down real healing work and helpful conversations about race.

White-wash. "To alter (something) in a way that favors, features, or caters to white people: such as to portray (the past) in a way that increases the prominence, relevance, or impact of white people and minimizes or misrepresents that of nonwhite people."[18]

Notes

Introduction

1. John R. Franke, *Missional Theology: An Introduction* (Grand Rapids: Baker Academic, 2020), 167.
2. Özlem Sensoy and Robin DiAngelo, *Is Everyone Really Equal?* (New York: Teachers College Press, 2017).
3. Sensoy and DiAngelo, 60.
4. Sensoy and DiAngelo, 60.
5. Emergence Church, "Statement on Racial Unity," *Deeper Study Blog,* September 4, 2020, https://emergencenj.org/blog/2020/09/04/statement-on -racial-unity.

Chapter 1: Leadership

1. Christine E. Sleeter, ed., call for papers for "Genealogy and Critical Family History," special issue of *Genealogy,* accessed October 2020, https://mdpi.com /journal/genealogy/special_issues/critical.
2. John 8:31–32.
3. I don't say "dark night of the soul" anymore because of the ways in which darkness is constructed to represent "bad." Rather, I want to express that deconstructing Whiteness is a journey into the depths of ourselves, the deep recesses that may be as yet unexplored. As such, "deep midnight" feels better than perpetuating some sort of false equivalency of darkness = bad.
4. Naledi Ushe, "Sheryl Underwood Opens Up about Exchange with Sharon Osbourne about Piers Morgan," *People,* March 12, 2021, https://people.com/tv sheryl-underwood-opens-up-exchange-sharon-osbourne-piers-morgan/.
5. Luke 10:7.

Chapter 2: Preaching and Liturgy

1. Owe Wikström, "Liturgy as Experience—The Psychology of Worship: A Theoretical and Empirical Lacuna," *Scripta Instituti Donneriani Aboensis* 15 (1993): 83–100.
2. Lillian Smith, *A Lillian Smith Reader,* ed. Margaret Rose Gladney and Lisa Hodgens (Athens: The University of Georgia Press, 2016), 80.

3. James Small and Salim Adofo, "Journey to the Motherland," YouTube video, August 20, 2017, https://www.youtube.com/watch?v=F6jrUPIlpOE&t=393s.

4. Small and Adofo.

5. Bill Moyers, *Bill Moyers Journal: The Conversation Continues* (New York: New Press, 2011), 528.

6. Laurens de Rooij and Joanildo Burity, "Liberation Theology," in *SAGE Encyclopedia of Economics and Society*, ed. Frederick F. Wherry and Juliet B. Schor (Los Angeles: SAGE Publications, 2015).

7. James Cone, "The Relationship of the Christian Faith to Political Praxis" (speech, Princeton Theological Seminary, Princeton, NJ, March 12, 1980), available at *American Radioworks,* http://americanradioworks.publicradio.org/features /blackspeech/jcone.html.

8. Mary McClintock Fulkerson and Marcia W. Mount Shoop, *A Body Broken, A Body Betrayed: Race, Memory, and Eucharist in White-Dominant Churches* (Eugene, OR: Cascade Books, 2015), 3.

9. Fulkerson and Shoop, 3.

10. Fulkerson and Shoop, 23.

Chapter 3: Music

1. Shirley Erena Murray, "For Everyone Born, a Place at the Table" (Carol Stream, IL: Hope Publishing, 1998).

2. Euronews, "Hong Kong Protesters Chant 'Do You Hear the People Sing?,'" June 17, 2019, YouTube video, https://www.youtube.com/watch?v =LiFpZ9OOEe0.

3. Kathleen M. Higgins, "Connecting Music to Ethics," *College Music Symposium* 58, no. 3 (Fall 2018): 1–20.

4. Higgins, 5, 6.

5. Christy Nockels and Nathan Nockels, "A Mighty Fortress" (Capitol CMG Publishing, 2009).

6. Daniel C. Roberts, "God of Our Fathers, Whose Almighty Hand," 1876.

7. "Church Choir Sings 'Make America Great Again' Song," ABC News, July 4, 2017, https://abcnews.go.com/US/video/church-choir-sings-make-america -great-song-48438840.

8. David O. Stewart, review of *Snow-Storm in August: Washington City, Francis Scott Key, and the Forgotten Race Riot of 1835,* by Jefferson Morley, *Washington Post*, July 27, 2012, https://www.washingtonpost.com/opinion/snow-storm-in -august-by-jefferson-morley/2012/07/27/gJQA7eJcEX_story.html.

9. Jefferson Morley, "Even Republicans Should Care about the Racist History of 'The Star-Spangled Banner,'" *Washington Post*, August 28, 2020, https://www .washingtonpost.com/outlook/2020/08/28/even-republicans-should-care-about -racist-history-star-spangled-banner/.

10. Burton W. Peretti, "Lift Ev'ry Voice and Sing," https://www.loc.gov/static /programs/national-recording-preservation-board/documents/LiftEveryVoice AndSing.pdf.

11. Mark Medley, "Subversive Song: Imagining Colossians 1:15–20 as a Social Protest Hymn in the Context of Roman Empire," *Review and Expositor* 116, no. 4 (November 2019): 421–35.

12. James Weldon Johnson, "Lift Every Voice and Sing" in *Complete Poems: Johnson* (New York: Penguin Books, 2000).

13. "Behind the Lyrics of 'Lift Every Voice and Sing,'" CNN. https://www .cnn.com/interactive/2020/09/us/lift-every-voice-and-sing-trnd/.

14. Medley, "Subversive Song," 428.

15. Medley, 423.

16. Mark A. Miller, "Child of God" (Dallas: Choristers Guild, 2014).

17. Medley, "Subversive Song."

18. Medley, 428.

19. Dan Damon, quoted in Nancy E. Hall, "Singing Our Way to Justice: A Conversation with Dan Damon—Hymn Writer, Composer, and Pastor," *Review and Expositor* 114, no. 3 (August 2017): 403–13 (408).

20. 1 Corinthians 13:1.

21. Sandra Maria Van Opstal, *The Next Worship: Glorifying God in a Diverse World* (Downers Grove, IL: InterVarsity Press, 2016), 20–23.

Chapter 4: Small Groups

1. Cecilia L. Ridgeway and Tamar Kricheli-Katz, "Intersecting Cultural Beliefs in Social Relations: Gender, Race, and Class Binds and Freedoms," *Gender and Society* 27, no. 3 (June 2013): 294–318.

2. Ridgeway and Kricheli-Katz.

3. Richard M. Emerson, "Power-Dependence Relations," *American Sociological Review* 27, no. 1 (February 1962): 35.

4. Emerson, 35.

5. Mike Breen, *Building a Discipling Culture,* 3rd ed. (Greenville, SC: 3DM International, 2017).

Chapter 5: Buildings and Grounds

1. Kerry Connelly, *Good White Racist? Confronting Your Role in Racial Injustice* (Louisville, KY: Westminster John Knox Press, 2020), 103.

2. Connelly, 103.

3. Bull City 150, "Dismantling Hayti," accessed June 9, 2021, https://www .bullcity150.org/uneven_ground/dismantling_hayti/.

4. Jessica Caporuscio, "What Are Food Deserts, and How Do They Impact Health?," *Medical News Today,* June 22, 2020, https://www.medicalnewstoday .com/articles/what-are-food-deserts#location.

5. "Gentrification and the Black Church in New York City," *Red Hook Star-Revue,* August 11, 2020, www.star-revue.com/gentrification-and-the-black -church/.

6. "Old Redford History," accessed April 14, 2021, http://mauraseale.org /public-history/exhibits/show/detroit-1945-to-now/race-and-redlining.

7. Henry Louis Gates Jr., "To Understand America, You Need to Understand the Black Church," *Time,* February 17, 2021, https://time.com/5939921/henry -lous-gates-american-history-black-church/.

8. Quoted in Gates.

9. Gates.

10. Christina Zanfagna, "Under the Blasphemous W(RAP): Locating the 'Spirit' in Hip-Hop," *Pacific Review of Ethnomusicology* 12 (2006), https://ethno musicologyreview.ucla.edu/journal/volume/12/piece/507.

11. Kenneth V. Hardy, "Healing the Hidden Wounds of Racial Trauma," *Reclaiming Children and Youth* 22, no. 1 (Spring 2013): 24–28, https://static1 .squarespace.com/static/545cdfcce4b0a64725b9f65a/t/54da3451e4b0ac9bd1d1 cd30/1423586385564/Healing.pdf.

12. Hardy.

13. Bill McGraw, "Bring Detroit's Black Bottom Back to (Virtual) Life," *Detroit Free Press*, February 27, 2017.

14. Adam Fairclough, "The Costs of *Brown*: Black Teachers and School Integration," *Journal of American History* 91, no. 1 (June 2004): 44–45, https://doi .org/10.2307/3659612.

Chapter 6: Communications

1. Emily McFarlan Miller, "Texas United Methodists Take Up Call to Replace Denomination's Logo over Association with Racist Imagery," *Religion News Service,* September 23, 2020, https://religionnews.com/2020/09/23/texas -united-methodists-take-up-call-to-replace-denominations-logo-over-association -with-racist-imagery/.

2. DeNeen L. Brown, "The Preacher Who Used Christianity to Revive the Ku Klux Klan," *Washington Post,* April 10, 2018, https://www.washingtonpost.com /news/retropolis/wp/2018/04/08/the-preacher-who-used-christianity-to-revive -the-ku-klux-klan/.

3. James Baldwin and Werner Kracht, *Notes of a Native Son* (Dortmund: Lensing, 1965), 6.

4. DeeDee Roe, "Captive Audience: A Black Woman's Reflection on the Sparrow Conference," *Witness,* April 2, 2019, https://thewitnessbcc.com/captive -audience/.

5. Nicola A. Menzie, "Comments about 'Whiteness' Prompt Controversy at Sparrow Women Conference," *Religion News Service,* April 6, 2019, https:// religionnews.com/2019/04/06/comments-about-whiteness-prompt-walkout-at -sparrow-women-conference/.

6. Darian Symoné Harvin, "Skin Whitening Products Get a Rebrand, but It Doesn't Erase Centuries of Colorism," *Allure,* September 14, 2020, https://www .allure.com/story/end-of-skin-whitening-products.

7. Harvin.

8. Bethany Allen-Ebrahimian, "Study: Hollywood Casts More Light-Skinned Actors for Chinese Market," *Axios,* September 8, 2020, https://www.axios.com /hollywood-casting-china-colorism-light-skinned-df469d97-66c2-4b33-b41e -1feb29bf1f75.html.

9. Rob McLean, "Heineken Pulls 'Sometimes Lighter Is Better' Ad after Racism Claims," CNN, March 27, 2018, https://money.cnn.com/2018/03/27 /news/companies/heineken-pulls-ad-racism-accusations/index.html.

Chapter 7: Missions and Service

1. Camara Phyllis Jones, *Racial Equity Training,* 2013, https://www.racial equityinstitute.com/groundwaterapproach.

Chapter 8: Children and Youth

1. A brief definition of this phrase can be found in the glossary. For a full discussion of the term, see Kerry Connelly, *Good White Racist? Confronting Your Role in Racial Injustice* (Louisville, KY: Westminster John Knox Press, 2020).

2. W. M. Liu et al., "Racial Trauma, Microaggressions, and Becoming Racially Innocuous: The Role of Acculturation and White Supremacist Ideology," *American Psychologist* 74, no. 1 (2019): 143–55.

3. Liu et al., 149.

4. Judith H. Katz, "The Sociopolitical Nature of Counseling," *Counseling Psychologist* 13, no. 4 (1985): 618, quoted in Liu et al., 146.

5. Bryana Clover, "Crossing the Line from Labels to Identity." November 5, 2020, https://www.bryanaclover.com/post/crossing-the-line-from-labels-to -identity. For an overview of the history of Black hair, see Tabora A. Johnson and Teiahsha Bankhead, "Hair It Is: Examining the Experiences of Black Women with Natural Hair," *Open Journal of Social Sciences* 2, no. 1 (January 2014): 86–100.

6. Adia Harvey Wingfield, "Being Black—but Not Too Black—in the Workplace," *Atlantic,* October 14, 2015, https://www.theatlantic.com/business /archive/2015/10/being-black-work/409990/.

7. Megan Trimble, "These States Still Had Active KKK Groups in 2017," *U.S. News & World Report,* August 14, 2017.

8. "In 2020, We Tracked 54 Hate Groups in Texas," Southern Poverty Law Center, accessed April 15, 2021, https://www.splcenter.org/hate-map?state=TX.

9. Brittany Packnett, "Ally, Accomplice, Co-conspirator," June 13, 2019, YouTube video, https://www.youtube.com/watch?v=QZVILjJPreM.

10. Derald Wing Sue et al., "Disarming Racial Microaggressions: Microintervention Strategies for Targets, White Allies, and Bystanders," *American Psychologist* 74, no. 1 (2019): 128–42.

11. Sue et al., 133.

12. Kevin Nadal, interview by Andrew Limbong, *NPR,* June 9, 2020, https://www.npr.org/2020/06/08/872371063/microaggressions-are-a-big-deal-how-to-talk-them-out-and-when-to-walk-away.

Chapter 9: Pastoral Care

1. Saira Mohamed, "Of Monsters and Men: Perpetrator Trauma and Mass Atrocity," *Columbia Law Review* 115, no. 5 (June 2015): 1170.

2. Mohamed, 1173.

3. Nicole LePera, *How to Do the Work: Recognize Your Patterns, Heal from Your Past, and Create Your Self* (New York: Harper Wave, 2021), 44.

4. LePera, 45.

5. LePera, 45.

6. Thandeka, *Learning to Be White: Money, Race, and God in America* (New York: Continuum, 1999).

7. Mohamed, "Of Monsters and Men," 1176.

8. LePera, *How to Do the Work,* 45.

9. Rebecca Traister, "Andrew Cuomo and the Performance of Power," interview, *Ezra Klein Show* (podcast), *New York Times,* March 19, 2021.

Conclusion: Your Plan of Action

1. "What Is RACI? An Introduction," RACI Solutions, https://www.racisolutions.com/blog/what-is-raci-an-introduction.

Glossary

1. Brittany Packnett, "Ally, Accomplice, Co-conspirator," June 13, 2019, YouTube video, https://www.youtube.com/watch?v=QZVILjJPreM.

2. Packnett.

3. Packnett.

4. Packnett.

5. Brown University, "How Structural Racism Works: Tricia Rose," December 14, 2015, YouTube video, www.youtube.com/watch?v=KT1vsOJctMk.

6. Richard M. Emerson, "Power-Dependence Relations," *American Sociological Review* 27, no. 1 (February 1962): 35.

7. Lexico.com, s.v. "cultural appropriation," accessed August 11, 2021, https://www.lexico.com/definition/cultural_appropriation.

8. Roderick Thomas, "Gentrification and the Black Church in New York City," *Red Hook Star-Revue,* August 11, 2020, www.star-revue.com/gentrification -and-the-black-church/.

9. Özlem Sensoy and Robin DiAngelo, *Is Everyone Really Equal?* (New York: Teachers College Press, 2017), 91.

10. Lexico.com, s.v. "microaggression," accessed August 5, 2021, https:// www.lexico.com/en/definition/microaggression.

11. Sensoy and DiAngelo, *Is Everyone Really Equal?*, 54.

12. W. M. Liu et al., "Racial Trauma, Microaggressions, and Becoming Racially Innocuous: The Role of Acculturation and White Supremacist Ideology," *American Psychologist* 74, no. 1 (2019): 149.

13. Terry Gross, "A 'Forgotten History' of How the U.S. Government Segregated America," *Fresh Air,* May 3, 2017, https://www.npr.org/2017/05/03/526655831/a -forgotten-history-of-how-the-u-s-government-segregated-america.

14. Sensoy and DiAngelo, *Is Everyone Really Equal?*, 60.

15. Saira Mohamed, "Of Monsters and Men: Perpetrator Trauma and Mass Atrocity," *Columbia Law Review* 115, no. 5 (June 2015): 1170.

16. Judith H. Katz, "The Sociopolitical Nature of Counseling," *Counseling Psychologist* 13, no. 4 (1985): 618, quoted in Liu et al., 146.

17. Urban Dictionary, s.v. "White savior," last modified March 8, 2012, l.

18. *Merriam-Webster,* s.v. "whitewash," accessed August 11, 2021, https:// www.merriam-webster.com/dictionary/whitewash.

CPSIA information can be obtained
at www.ICGtesting.com
Printed in the USA
BVHW041759150222
629097BV00008B/54

9 780664 267506